T0209414

An Analysis of

# Hannah Arendt's

# The Human Condition

Sahar Aurore Saeidnia
with
Anthony Lang

Published by Macat International Ltd
24:13 Coda Centre, 189 Munster Road, London SW6 6AW.

Distributed exclusively by Routledge
2 Park Square, Milton Park, Abingdon, Oxon OX14 4RN
711 Third Avenue, New York, NY 10017, USA

*Routledge is an imprint of the Taylor & Francis Group, an informa business*

www.macat.com
info@macat.com

*Cataloguing in Publication Data*
A catalogue record for this book is available from the British Library.
Library of Congress Cataloguing-in-Publication Data is available upon request.
Cover illustration: Etienne Gilfillan

ISBN 978-1-912302-94-9 (hardback)
ISBN 978-1-912127-88-7 (paperback)
ISBN 978-1-912281-82-4 (e-book)

**Notice**
The information in this book is designed to orientate readers of the work under analysis,
to elucidate and contextualise its key ideas and themes, and to aid in the development
of critical thinking skills. It is not meant to be used, nor should it be used, as a
substitute for original thinking or in place of original writing or research. References and
notes are provided for informational purposes and their presence does not constitute
endorsement of the information or opinions therein. This book is presented solely for
educational purposes. It is sold on the understanding that the publisher is not engaged
to provide any scholarly advice. The publisher has made every effort to ensure that
this book is accurate and up-to-date, but makes no warranties or representations with
regard to the completeness or reliability of the information it contains. The information
and the opinions provided herein are not guaranteed or warranted to produce particular
results and may not be suitable for students of every ability. The publisher shall not be
liable for any loss, damage or disruption arising from any errors or omissions, or from
the use of this book, including, but not limited to, special, incidental, consequential or
other damages caused, or alleged to have been caused, directly or indirectly, by the
information contained within.

# CONTENTS

# THE MACAT LIBRARY

The Macat Library is a series of unique academic explorations of seminal works in the humanities and social sciences – books and papers that have had a significant and widely recognised impact on their disciplines. It has been created to serve as much more than just a summary of what lies between the covers of a great book. It illuminates and explores the influences on, ideas of, and impact of that book. Our goal is to offer a learning resource that encourages critical thinking and fosters a better, deeper understanding of important ideas.

Each publication is divided into three Sections: Influences, Ideas, and Impact. Each Section has four Modules. These explore every important facet of the work, and the responses to it.

This Section-Module structure makes a Macat Library book easy to use, but it has another important feature. Because each Macat book is written to the same format, it is possible (and encouraged!) to cross-reference multiple Macat books along the same lines of inquiry or research. This allows the reader to open up interesting interdisciplinary pathways.

To further aid your reading, lists of glossary terms and people mentioned are included at the end of this book (these are indicated by an asterisk [*] throughout) – as well as a list of works cited.

Macat has worked with the University of Cambridge to identify the elements of critical thinking and understand the ways in which six different skills combine to enable effective thinking.
Three allow us to fully understand a problem; three more give us the tools to solve it. Together, these six skills make up the **PACIER** model of critical thinking. They are:

**ANALYSIS** – understanding how an argument is built
**EVALUATION** – exploring the strengths and weaknesses of an argument
**INTERPRETATION** – understanding issues of meaning

**CREATIVE THINKING** – coming up with new ideas and fresh connections
**PROBLEM-SOLVING** – producing strong solutions
**REASONING** – creating strong arguments

To find out more, visit **WWW.MACAT.COM.**

# CRITICAL THINKING AND *THE HUMAN CONDITION*

## Primary critical thinking skill: INTERPRETATION
## Secondary critical thinking skill: CREATIVE THINKING

Hannah Arendt's 1958 work *The Human Condition* was an impassioned philosophical reconsideration of the goals of being human.

In its arguments about the kind of lives we should lead and the political engagement we should strive for, Arendt's interpretative skills come to the fore in a brilliant display of what high-level interpretation can achieve for critical thinking. Good interpretative thinkers are characterised by their ability to clarify meanings, question accepted definitions and posit good, clear definitions that allow their other critical thinking skills to take arguments deeper and further than most. In many ways, *The Human Condition* is all about definitions. Arendt's aim is to lay out an argument for political engagement and active participation in society as the highest goals of human life, and to this end she sets about defining a hierarchy of ways of living a "vita activa," or active life. The book sets about distinguishing between our different activities under the categories of "labor", "work", and "action" – each of which Arendt carefully redefines as a different level of active engagement with the world. Following her clear and careful setting out of each word's meaning, it becomes hard to deny her argument for the life of "action" as the highest human goal.

## ABOUT THE AUTHOR OF THE ORIGINAL WORK

One of the twentieth century's most influential thinkers, **Hannah Arendt** was born in 1906 to Jewish parents in Germany. Her family did not raise her to be religious, but with the growth of anti-Semitism, Jewishness became more central to her identity. She received her PhD in philosophy from Heidelberg University in 1926 and left Germany in 1933. After a brief imprisonment in France during World War II, Arendt immigrated to the United States. Living primarily in New York city, she taught at universities across the country and lectured around the world. She died in 1975 at the age of 69.

## ABOUT THE AUTHORS OF THE ANALYSIS

**Sahar Aurore Saeidnia** is a doctoral candidate in sociology at the Ecole des Hautes Etudes en Sciences Sociales, Paris.

**Dr Anthony Lang** is Head of the School of International Relations at the University of St Andrews. His work focuses on questions of agency, responsibility and punishment in political theory.

## ABOUT MACAT

### GREAT WORKS FOR CRITICAL THINKING

Macat is focused on making the ideas of the world's great thinkers accessible and comprehensible to everybody, everywhere, in ways that promote the development of enhanced critical thinking skills.

It works with leading academics from the world's top universities to produce new analyses that focus on the ideas and the impact of the most influential works ever written across a wide variety of academic disciplines. Each of the works that sit at the heart of its growing library is an enduring example of great thinking. But by setting them in context – and looking at the influences that shaped their authors, as well as the responses they provoked – Macat encourages readers to look at these classics and game-changers with fresh eyes. Readers learn to think, engage and challenge their ideas, rather than simply accepting them.

'Macat offers an amazing first-of-its-kind tool for interdisciplinary learning and research. Its focus on works that transformed their disciplines and its rigorous approach, drawing on the world's leading experts and educational institutions, opens up a world-class education to anyone.'

**Andreas Schleicher**
**Director for Education and Skills, Organisation for Economic Co-operation and Development**

'Macat is taking on some of the major challenges in university education … They have drawn together a strong team of active academics who are producing teaching materials that are novel in the breadth of their approach.'

**Prof Lord Broers,**
**former Vice-Chancellor of the University of Cambridge**

'The Macat vision is exceptionally exciting. It focuses upon new modes of learning which analyse and explain seminal texts which have profoundly influenced world thinking and so social and economic development. It promotes the kind of critical thinking which is essential for any society and economy. This is the learning of the future.'

**Rt Hon Charles Clarke, former UK Secretary of State for Education**

'The Macat analyses provide immediate access to the critical conversation surrounding the books that have shaped their respective discipline, which will make them an invaluable resource to all of those, students and teachers, working in the field.'

**Professor William Tronzo, University of California at San Diego**

# WAYS IN TO THE TEXT

## KEY POINTS

- German-born Hannah Arendt (1906–75) immigrated to the United States during World War II* (1939–45). Her work profoundly shaped modern political theory.

- Her book *The Human Condition* (1958) emphasizes political action and pluralism* (the idea that the various possible ways of being in the world should be respected); both remain central to politics today.

- *The Human Condition* argues that politics creates and recreates institutions that allow for democratic participation.

### Who Was Hannah Arendt?

Born in Germany in 1906, Hannah Arendt, the author of *The Human Condition* (1958), was one of the most influential political thinkers of the twentieth century. She studied philosophy with important figures such as Martin Heidegger,* the author of the renowned work *Being and Time* (1927), and Karl Jaspers,* the influential author of *Philosophy* (1932). As a Jew, she was forced to leave Germany in 1933 when the ruling Nazi* Party refused to allow Jews to hold meaningful jobs. She spent some time in Paris supporting Jews who were trying to immigrate to Palestine. After a brief internment in a French refugee camp, she eventually moved to the United States with her husband,

Heinrich Blucher,* a philosopher and Marxist* thinker. Marxism is a set of political and economic theories developed in the mid to late nineteenth century; it explains social change in terms of economics, and predicts a workers' revolution that will overthrow the social and economic system of capitalism.* Arendt and Blucher worked primarily in New York city.

Arendt published books and essays on topics such as revolution, political action, freedom, power, and authority. Providing the theoretical foundation for her overall approach to political life, *The Human Condition* (1958) remains the most important of her works— but not just in terms of understanding Arendt. The text emphasizes action over passivity in political life. Instead of seeing politics as being about governments serving the people, Arendt argues that true politics is about active citizenship. Individuals must come together to recreate their institutions through constant action, such as revolutions or political protests.

Arendt first came to the attention of the reading public with the publication of *The Origins of Totalitarianism* in 1951. After *The Human Condition,* she wrote a number of other influential works. In 1961, the *New Yorker* magazine asked her to report on the war crimes trial of the Nazi bureaucrat Adolf Eichmann,* who was charged with organizing the transportation of Jewish people to concentration camps, and who was tried in Israel. She expanded the article into a book, *Eichmann in Jerusalem* (1963). In it, she coined the phrase "the banality of evil" to describe how unthinking bureaucrats could sanction horrific events. She also described how the Nazi bureaucracy used European Jewish community institutions to facilitate the transfer of Jews to their deaths. This caused a great deal of controversy among Jewish readers. In 1963, she published *On Revolution,* an influential comparison of the American Revolution* of 1775–81, which ended with the establishment of the United States, and the French Revolution* of 1789–93, which saw the overthrow of the monarchy and the creation

of a republic. She also wrote significant essays about civil disobedience*
(action, usually peaceful but unlawful, taken to protest against a
government), violence, power, and authority. In her later years, Arendt
turned to what she called "the life of the mind," seeking to understand
three things: thinking, willing, and judging. She died in 1975 at the
age of 69 while writing about the final subject, judging.

## What Does *The Human Condition* Say?

*The Human Condition* proposes that human life is defined by three
kinds of activity: labor, work, and action. Labor includes what we do
to support our daily needs, such as feeding ourselves. Work includes
things that will outlive our immediate lives, such as science, art, and
literature. Action remains the quintessentially political form of activity;
it allows us to work together to shape our common destiny. Arendt
believed action to be important and all too neglected in our
understanding of "normal politics." While some see political life as
being about purely economic schemes or social debates, Arendt
believed politics should primarily be about how people work in
unison to create new institutions. These new institutions in turn create
spaces in which we can reveal ourselves in public to each other.

The book is an example of what is called a phenomenological*
approach to politics. Phenomenology is a philosophical study of the
structures of subjective experience and consciousness ("subjective
experience" here means, simply, experience belonging uniquely to an
individual). *The Human Condition* focuses on the realm of appearances,
rather than a search for some fundamental truth about human life or
politics. Action, which Arendt saw as the most important form of
human activity, is partly about creating new institutions. But it is also
about revealing ourselves to each other in a commonly constructed
political space.

Modern politics too often neglects this activity of public revelation,
or misunderstands it, thinking it means revealing things about our

personal lives. But Arendt would label our personal lives as belonging to the social realm rather than the political realm. Revealing ourselves in political life means advancing ideas and creating institutions through which we can accept a plurality of visions of how politics should function. Pluralism is the idea that there are many different ways of being in the world, that they should all be respected, and that we can benefit from these alternative views and ideas.

The book also draws heavily on a particular reading of the ancient Greek* experience—both the history of democracy as we understand it from its origins in the Greek city of Athens, and the ideas of the Greek philosopher Aristotle.* Aristotle defined human beings as thinking, political actors. Arendt emphasized the political element of human life even more than the thinking part. This suggests she believed philosophers like the Greek philosopher Plato,* who saw humans as primarily thinkers, to have been mistaken.

*The Human Condition* argues against Marxist theories. Arendt believed they focused too much attention on the realm of labor, while neglecting the realm of political action. The book also positions itself against forms of the political philosophy of liberalism,* which see politics as being about giving maximum freedom to individuals to pursue their personal interests. Arendt did believe in the protection of a private space for individuals, but she also believed that politics should be about acting together and becoming proud citizens of our respective countries.

The book introduces or redefines important concepts. The idea of plurality, for instance, represents more than liberal pluralism.* It focuses more on creating spaces for a large number of different forms of citizen engagement. Arendt also created the idea of natality,* the idea that politics always centers on giving birth to new institutions and ideas.

The book begins and ends by reminding us that we are bound to this planet. Our human existence cannot be about afterlives or other worlds. Instead, we must focus our politics in the here and now. Doing so will give us the means to continually improve *the human condition* as we create new spaces and institutions to make our common life easier.

## Why Does *The Human Condition* Matter?

*The Human Condition* remains just as relevant today as it was in 1958. The totalitarian* regimes of Nazi Germany, the Soviet Union,* and Eastern Europe that concerned Arendt so much during her lifetime may have now disappeared—totalitarianism is a political system in which the centralized government holds total authority over society, controls private and public life, and requires complete subservience— but in the twenty-first century, states and multinational companies govern and control us through surveillance and technology. These forms of control turn us into passive consumers. *The Human Condition* reminds us how important it is to be active, to *engage* in a life of politics in which we can resist things we don't want or like, and create new institutions. The book emphasizes the benefits of political activism, such as the popular revolts in the Middle East of 2010 collectively known as the Arab Spring.* Even when those movements collapse or fail, they are examples of *the human condition* of continual striving to resist and to create new political institutions and ideas.

*The Human Condition*'s emphasis on the world of appearances (abstract subjective experiences rather than fundamental truths) also makes it relevant today. A focus on the otherworldly concerns of religions has crept into politics in many regions of the world. Arendt believed, rather, that we are bound by the earth on which we live. That means we must act together to succeed in navigating the tensions that arise from living in a crowded space. Instead of hoping for utopias either here or elsewhere, we must conduct politics in *this* world. That means creating space for disagreement and conflict in ways that do not lead to violence.

Finally, and connected to the last point, Arendt's emphasis on plurality and respect for others helps the work move past simple liberal platitudes about accepting others, and toward a more active approach to shaping politics. Unlike tolerance, which means grudgingly accepting others, pluralism means actively embracing differences and appreciating others for what they can bring to politics. Arendt's work reminds us of how important it is not simply to tolerate difference, but to embrace plurality.

# SECTION 1
# INFLUENCES

# THE AUTHOR AND THE HISTORICAL CONTEXT

## KEY POINTS

- Hannah Arendt's *The Human Condition* helps us see the importance of political action in the face of forces that seek to limit our engagement with the world and with each other.

- *The Human Condition* arose from the author's education as a student of German philosophy in the early twentieth century, and from her experience of being a Jew in Nazi* Germany.

- *The Human Condition* continued her work on totalitarianism* (a political system with a domineering centralized government) and articulates an idea of politics that emphasizes action as the defining element of *the human condition*.

### Why Read this Text?

Hannah Arendt's *The Human Condition* (1958) remains an important text more than half a century after its publication. While politics can lead to conflict, Arendt emphasized the plurality* of our life on this earth: we can benefit, she argues, from alternative views and ideas, and we must respect and work with others to create new political institutions. Both religious and secular* fundamentalist* ideologies (belief systems that seek to return to the "fundamentals" or most important elements of a tradition) fail to acknowledge this plurality. They assume that we possess only one human nature, which can be molded to create perfection. Arendt reminds us that while we share

> **66** In the early 1950s Hannah Arendt began to envision a new science of politics for a world in which political events, world wars, totalitarianism, and atomic bombing demanded serious attention from philosophers. **99**
>
> Elisabeth Young-Bruehl, *Hannah Arendt: For Love Of The World*

the earth, we do not share a single human nature. We must remake ourselves anew with each generation.

For Arendt, general philosophical principles cannot regulate the political domain. She seeks to reform political theory by underlining the contingency* of human life, and especially by defining action as the central concept of politics. "Contingency" is the idea that we cannot predict the possible outcome of any course of action. Arendt wrote *The Human Condition* in the aftermath of World War II,* when the world needed a new approach to politics. She brought a message of hope—that people remain active beings and that action enables us to create new things—that is still relevant today. Her work serves as a "reminder of the vital importance of politics, and of properly understanding our political capacities and the dangers and opportunities they offer."[1]

## Author's Life

Arendt was born in 1906 in the city of Linden (now Hanover) to a social democrat* family of secular German Jews; social democrats subscribe to liberal* principles of democracy and endorse economic policies that allow the fair distribution of wealth. She enrolled at Marburg University in 1924 to study under the influential German philosopher Martin Heidegger.* Arendt's education, with its focus on ancient history and philosophy, shaped her thinking. In 1926, she completed a doctoral degree in philosophy at Heidelberg University. The German Swiss philosopher Karl Jaspers* supervised her dissertation on the idea of love in the work of the early Christian theologian Augustine of Hippo.*

Partly because of the growth of anti-Semitism*—hostility and discrimination towards Jewish people—in Germany during her university years, Arendt's Jewish identity became more central to her thinking, and she associated herself with some Jewish and Zionist* organizations; Zionism is a nationalist and political movement that sees the land of Israel as the rightful homeland of the Jewish people.[2]

In 1933, the rise of Nazism forced Arendt to move to Paris, where she supported efforts to help Jews escape Europe, and worked in the resistance* (organizations that worked, violently and nonviolently, against the German occupation). After being imprisoned in 1941, Arendt escaped to the United States. She briefly returned to Germany at the end of the war to continue supporting Jewish refugees. She then returned to the United States, eventually becoming a US citizen. She and her husband Heinrich Blucher,* a philosopher and Marxist* thinker, lived largely in New York city, but Arendt taught at universities across the country and lectured widely around the world.

## Author's Background

Hannah Arendt's upbringing as a German Jew profoundly shaped her interest in politics, authority, and power. Her two early works—*The Origins of Totalitarianism* (1952) and *The Human Condition* (1958)—arose from her efforts to come to terms with the horrific events of two world wars. For her, the totalitarianism of Nazism and Stalinism* represented the end of common and plural life, and the death of politics. She saw the repression of the Hungarian Revolution* in the early 1950s—a spontaneous revolt against the communist* government put down by the tanks of the Soviet Union*—as equally tragic, as it undermined the ability of individual citizens to shape their destinies.

Her identity as a Jew shaped her 1963 book *Eichmann in Jerusalem*. After originally believing that Israel represented hope for the Jewish people, she became disillusioned by the way in which the Jewish state continued to use the mass murder of European Jews by the Nazis for nationalist* purposes. Her engagement with US political thought partly shaped her work *On Revolution* (1963). In her collection of essays *Crises of the Republic* (1970), she analyzed America's imperialist* foreign policy (that is, the US policy of extending its sphere of cultural and economic influence beyond its own shores) in the Vietnam War,* and examined how citizens should respond to it. The best-known essay in the collection, "On Violence," examines the decolonization* period, when former colonies of the European powers sought their independence. This took place largely in Africa, but Middle East and Asian colonies also sought independence during this period. It also looks at attempts by figures in the United States and elsewhere to justify violence in the context of revolution.

## NOTES

1   Hannah Arendt, *The Human Condition*, introduced by Margaret Canovan (Chicago: University of Chicago Press, 1998), xvi.

2   Some of her writings on Zionism and Judaism can be found in Hannah Arendt, *The Jewish Writings*, eds. Jerome Kohn and Ron H. Feldman (New York: Random House, 2006).

# MODULE 2
# ACADEMIC CONTEXT

## KEY POINTS

- Philosophy deals with understanding reality and existence.

- Contemplative philosophy,* an abstract and theoretical approach, has long been considered the best way to understand reality.

- Arendt rejects classical contemplative philosophy for a more active and concrete mode of thought. She underlines this rupture by calling herself a political theorist rather than a political philosopher.

### The Work In Its Context

Hannah Arendt published *The Human Condition* in 1958. The field of philosophy had been consistently dominated by a contemplative tradition that started with the ancient Greek* philosopher Plato.* Contemplative philosophy focuses on the life of the mind and prizes theoretical reflection over political action. This approach seeks a transcendental* truth (a term used to describe a reality that is beyond the observable or empirically verifiable) to explain the world. It considers thought the most valuable activity a person can engage in.

During Arendt's lifetime, most philosophers adopted one of two styles: analytic philosophy* or continental philosophy.*[1] To simplify the distinctions we can say that analytical philosophers think about reality with conceptual and argumentative clarity, objectivism* (the assumption that the mind and reality are independent), and logic. They often identify with the sciences and mathematics, rather than with the humanities. The foundational key figures of this tradition include the Austrian British philosopher Ludwig Wittgenstein* and the American

> ❝ *The Human Condition* questions the major Western tradition from Plato to Marx which sees humans coming to the full realization of their potential in the theoretical life. For Arendt this emphasis on the theoretical is a betrayal of the practical. ❞
>
> Dermot Moran, *Introduction to Phenomenology*

John Rawls.* In contrast, the theories of continental philosophers tend to be more literary and less analytical, and more interested in political, cultural, and metaphysical* issues (that is, abstract issues concerning the nature of reality, time, and so on). These philosophers often work from a historical perspective. Scholars usually consider the early nineteenth-century German philosopher Georg Wilhelm Friedrich Hegel* to have been the founder of this approach.

Other key figures (all German) in continental philosophy included the nineteenth-century founder of socialism, Karl Marx;* the philosopher Edmund Husserl,* whose work straddled the nineteenth and twentieth centuries; Martin Heidegger;* and Jürgen Habermas.* Analytic philosophy dominated in English-speaking countries during the twentieth century. As the name implies, philosophers throughout Europe more commonly practiced continental philosophy. But the geographical divide is misleading. The main differences between the two approaches lay in their methods and approaches.

### Overview of the Field
In the 1950s, when Arendt was working on *The Human Condition*, the analytical/continental debate turned into a debate between positivism* and phenomenology.*

In philosophy, positivism values empirical* data (that is, information acquired through observation) and scientific methods over metaphysical speculations. From a positivist perspective, we find truth by observing and interpreting factual data. Phenomenology, on the other hand, assumes that we cannot find truth by this means. Rather, all we have are "phenomena," or appearances. So we must focus on our subjective experiences, and the best we can do is understand reality as it appears to us. This philosophical tradition does not deny the existence of reality, but it suggests that simply "observing" and calculating will not reveal truths to us in the way that positivists believe they will.

Besides this classical split, ideological trends also divided the philosophical field. In the 1950s, the world was at the beginning of what would become a half-century of Cold War* struggle, a tense nuclear standoff between two superpowers—the US taking the side of democracy against the communist* Soviet Union.* This confrontation colored scholarship in many areas, including the social sciences. Indeed, the confrontation between liberal* traditions and Marxist* theories heavily influenced the ways in which scholars defined and answered philosophical problems. For instance, the liberal tradition usually speaks of individual freedoms (economic, social, and political). In Marxist theory, individuals find fulfillment via communal action designed to change the economic structures that surround us.

## Academic Influences

According to the English political theorist Margaret Canovan,* Arendt paid "no attention to mainstream debates" and always distrusted philosophical schools.[2] But in The Human Condition she drew on three of the greatest German philosophers of the twentieth century: Heidegger, Husserl, and Karl Jaspers.* In emphasizing the potential for political action to change the world around us, she drew on the phenomenological influences of Heidegger and Husserl. Like them, Arendt believed that we live in a world of appearances, so our actions can shape and reshape the world in fundamental ways. She shared Heidegger's perspective of "being in the world," which he had developed in his 1927 masterwork *Being and Time*.[3] Heidegger emphasized the importance of humans' interactions with their environment; but Arendt criticized his neglect of the cooperative dimension of human activity, because for her the world existed "between" people.[4] She rarely characterized herself as a phenomenologist, but we can understand her work as an offshoot of this tradition.

In criticizing the contemplative tradition of philosophy, Arendt echoed Jasper, who shared her tendency to gravitate toward a concrete and practical philosophy. Jasper introduced her to the eighteenth-century German philosopher Immanuel Kant's* reflection on politics. This led her to engage critically with ancient philosophers. She rejected Plato's political philosophy because it suggested—incorrectly, she thought—that philosophy remains superior to politics. Instead, she preferred Aristotle; in combining the active and philosophical life, she found his approach closer to her own. But Arendt went further than Aristotle in arguing for a politics of action above all else. She wanted to go beyond the contemplative tradition and renew thinking on politics. This contradicted both the predominant approach of American philosophers and mainstream European philosophy. She accused the latter of being incapable of understanding *the human condition* because it produced models disconnected from action. As a result, in the words of her biographer, "she had a deep suspicion of Hegelian* and Marxist attempts to explain the overall meaning of the historical as such."[5] ("Hegelian" refers to the philosophical approach of Hegel, focusing on how ideas determine our reality.)

This explains why Arendt was reluctant to call herself a philosopher and preferred the term "political theorist" or "political thinker."[6]

## NOTES

1   See Carl E. Schorske, "The New Rigorism in the Human Sciences, 1940–1960," *Daedelus* 126, no. 1 (1997): 289–310; and Brian Leiter and Michael Rosen, eds., *The Oxford Handbook of Continental Philosophy* (Oxford: Oxford University Press, 2007).

2   Margaret Canovan, introduction to *The Human Condition* by Hannah Arendt (Chicago: University of Chicago Press, 1998), xv.

3   Martin Heidegger, *Being and Time* (New York: Harper, 1962).

4   Hannah Arendt, *The Human Condition* (Chicago: University of Chicago Press, 1998), 52.

5   Dermot Moran, *Introduction to Phenomenology* (London & New York: Routledge, 2000), 290.

6   Elisabeth Young-Bruehl, *Hannah Arendt: For Love Of The World* (New Haven: Yale University Press, 2004), 327.

# MODULE 3
## THE PROBLEM

### KEY POINTS

- Arendt is concerned with the rise of the "social"—the idea that managerial and bureaucratic solutions can address all our problems.

- Politics should not be a matter of mere "housekeeping." It should create a public realm in which we can freely and robustly interact with each other.

- The rise of totalitarianism* is part of an overly managerial approach to politics that seeks to control everything we do, rather than liberate us to act on our own.

### Core Question

The core question Hannah Arendt addresses in *The Human Condition* is: How can political action prevent the dangers of totalitarianism? Arendt realized that deep problems in society and politics had created the conditions in which totalitarian politics could take root. She believed the core problem was a failure to understand the importance of political action in creating a public realm that allows all people to participate. This public realm should be separated in some deep way from the concerns of managing the economy and social problems. In her view, this core problem manifests itself in the importance of the "social," or a focus on societal needs rather than political problems and the disagreements they produce. She wanted to deemphasize the social and reemphasize what she thought of as the political, feeling that the contemplative* political philosophers of her generation— philosophers who followed an abstract and theoretical approach— failed to understand that reflections on truth and beauty cannot address the dangers of totalitarianism.

> ❝ ... the emergence of the social realm, which is neither private nor public, strictly speaking, is a relatively new phenomenon whose origin coincided with the emergence of the modern age and which found its political form in the nation-state. In our understanding, the dividing line [between these realms] is entirely blurred, because we see the body of peoples and political communities in the image of a family whose everyday affairs have to be taken care of by a gigantic, nation-wide administration of housekeeping. ❞
>
> Hannah Arendt, *The Human Condition*

To counter the dangers of Nazi* Germany or the communist* Soviet Union,* political action needed to be valued as a fundamental part of human life. Unlike the German political philosopher Karl Marx,* Arendt did not believe that the solution lay in creating new forms of economic distribution or new social rules. Rather, she believed people could resist creating new rules by focusing more on truly participatory political practices. Her originality lay in the distinction between the social and political. She argued that to prevent the rise of totalitarian politics, society needed to pay more attention to the political realm.

## The Participants
Concerned about the managerial and controlling approach that pervaded politics, Arendt first examined its roots in the classical contemplative tradition embodied in the work of the foundational philosopher Plato.* Plato believed that only philosophers should govern. But Arendt preferred a more participatory approach to politics, noting: "The Platonic* separation of knowing and doing has remained at the root of all theories of domination."[1]

Arendt also argued against political and social scientists who believed that managing and controlling populations was the best way to prevent totalitarianism. In the United States, liberal* economists and political scientists such as John Kenneth Galbraith* and W. W. Rostow* argued that the only role politics needed to play was controlling the economy. Other contemporary political scientists such as Charles Merriam* and David Easton* argued that this managerial approach translated political life into statistics and mathematical models. The Austrian British philosopher Karl Popper,* a contemporary of Arendt's, made a similar point. In his 1945 work *The Open Society and Its Enemies*, Popper argued that theorists from Plato through Karl Marx had distrusted the practice of democracy. They did so, in his view, because they feared that democracy might arrive at the "wrong" answers. The British philosopher Bernard Crick's* influential 1959 book *The American Science of Politics* offered yet another view of the contemporary situation, criticizing the managerial and economics-focused study of politics. Arendt shared his concerns.

## The Contemporary Debate

In contrast to her contemporaries, Arendt followed a unique line of thought. She sought to present a new form of politics that did not rely on managing society or economics. We may see this partly as a reaction to the rise of behavioralism,* which was just coming to the fore in political science, sociology, and economics; as its name implies, this approach to the study of social and political life focused on the analysis of individual behaviors. But as Arendt saw it, not all behaviors arise from the individual. Some actions, especially in the political realm, can arise unpredictably from communal desires. Revolutions and protest movements fall into this category. Other "actions" take the form of the institutions and structures that arise from those radical forms of politics. Behavioralism led analysts to focus more on statistics and management practices rather than on democracy, disagreement, and debate in political life. Arendt saw these behavioralist ideas as the heritage of the Platonic approach to politics. They disenfranchise people (deny them their rights) by allowing government to control their daily lives. Arendt also targeted Karl Marx, arguing that he focused his political theories solely on economic factors. Marx argued that we should interpret all political ideas and actions as arising from the economic structures created by capitalism.* Although Marxists and behavioralists represent very different ideological positions, both argued in favor of replacing the political sphere with the economic.

## NOTES

1    Hannah Arendt, *The Human Condition* (Chicago: University of Chicago Press, 1998), 225.

# MODULE 4
# THE AUTHOR'S CONTRIBUTION

## KEY POINTS

- Arendt emphasizes the importance of action and appearance, which can only be found in the political realm.

- In *The Human Condition* Arendt lays the foundation for an active philosophy, which she also defines as a political way to philosophize.

- Arendt uses the experience of ancient Greek* democracy to construct a phenomenological* analysis of politics and to investigate *the human condition*—that is, an analysis that begins with subjective experience and consciousness.

### Author's Aims

In *The Human Condition*, Hannah Arendt aimed to investigate conditions of both human existence and human activity. Some see philosophical reflection as the most important activity in human life, but she argued that political action remains most important of all: the act of coming together as a people to create institutions in a participatory and democratic manner. And how does she define "action"? In a particularly original way: "Action, the only activity that goes on directly between men without the intermediary of things or matter, corresponds to *the human condition* of plurality,* to the fact that men, not Man, inhabit the world. While all aspects of *the human condition* are somehow related to politics, this plurality is specifically the condition—not only the *conditio sine qua non** but the *conditio per quam** of all political life."[1]

In other words: plurality is both the cause and the engine of political life, and the most important things humans can do are to

> 66 Arendt's *The Human Condition*, first published in 1958, offers a careful phenomenological account of the nature of human action, situating it in the public realm, drawing heavily on Aristotle and using an idealised model of the Greek city-state or *polis*. 99
>
> Dermot Moran, *Introduction to Phenomenology*

come together purposefully, to respect each other, and to try to create new institutions that exist for the good of all. These actions fundamentally define humans in a way that separates them from other animals. For Arendt, contemporary philosophy ignores this plurality, which she saw as the fundamental condition of human beings. Arendt defined plurality as the condition of living with and respecting the views and actions of others.

In *The Human Condition*, Arendt proposes a new approach to politics. Reacting against the abstract notion of humanity that reduces all people to the same type with the same interests and concerns, Arendt's approach accepts the world as it is: a place filled with many kinds of people with differing interests and concerns. For Arendt, politics is not just about governing or organizing economic and social relations. It is about living with others, acting with others, and creating something new.

## Approach

Arendt became the first scholar to address the contemporary problems of totalitarianism* and democracy by analyzing the experience of democracy in ancient Greece over 2,000 years earlier. But she did not simply apply that model to contemporary politics. Instead, she used it as an inspiration for how we might encourage the creation of a new form of politics. By looking at modern politics through the history and ideas of the ancient world, she demonstrated the continuing relevance of the history of political thought. She also undertook a careful and critical analysis of the modern day. And she added a unique twist, moving away from the dry reflections of contemplative philosophy* to examine the potential of political action. No one else debating what modern democracy should look like took this approach.

*The Human Condition*'s first chapter starts with a general explanation of the *vita activa** ("active life") and explores Arendt's general approach and aims. She identifies the different activities that constitute an active life—labor, work, and action. The next chapter focuses on the spaces (public and private) in which the three different human activities take place. The next three chapters examine these activities. She concludes with "The *Vita Activa* and the Modern Age," a chapter dedicated to analyzing the modern world using her theoretical framework.

## Contribution in Context

The ideas developed in *The Human Condition* draw on a range of philosophical ideas and traditions, although Arendt's approach remained unique. The main theme—the *vita activa*—was directly inspired by the philosopher Aristotle's* concept of bios *politikos* ("political life") and the notion of *praxis** (roughly, "action") that he developed in his classic *Nichomachean Ethics*.[2] While classicists and historians of political thought dealt with Aristotle in the context of his own era, Arendt sought to make his ideas relevant to the modern day. She did this not by replicating all his ideas, but by using them to reorient political theory away from the search for truth and toward the search for successful democratic models. Arendt's encounters with phenomenology through her teachers Martin Heidegger* and Karl Jaspers* nourished her reflection about the idea of being in the world ("worldliness"), or the way human beings relate to the human world. Following Heidegger and Jaspers, Arendt focused on the description of the historical and existential* dimensions of the human experience (existentialism is a philosophical approach that emphasizes the lack of any governing order to the universe or reality). For her, "humanity should not be considered to have a permanent essential nature but only a certain condition."[3]

Arendt differentiated herself from Heidegger by inverting the traditional importance given to the *vita contemplativa** ("contemplative life") over the *vita activa*. She also criticized Heidegger's "neglect of cooperative human activity."[4] This exemplifies the originality of her approach. Heidegger believed that a philosopher should seek truth through reflection and avoid the messy world of practical politics. In Arendt's view, this allowed him to continue his pursuit of philosophy even as the world around him collapsed into war. In *The Human Condition*, she sought to reassert political activity as the most important activity in human life. She also wanted to create a practical work, looking toward the future. The keystone of her work lies in the distinction between the three activities—labor, work, and action. She developed this while reflecting on Marxist* contributions to the totalitarian experience and as a reaction against his concepts of political action and labor.

## NOTES

1   Hannah Arendt, *The Human Condition* (Chicago: University of Chicago Press, 1998), 7.

2   Aristotle, *Nicomachean Ethics*, trans. Martin Ostwald (New York: Macmillan, 1962).

3   Dermot Moran, *Introduction to Phenomenology* (London & New York: Routledge, 2000), 306.

4   Moran, *Introduction to Phenomenology*, 288.

# SECTION 2
## IDEAS

# MAIN IDEAS

## KEY POINTS

- Labor, work, and action are the three activities fundamental to *the human condition*, action being the central political activity.

- Politics arises when human beings act among and with others and create something new.

- Based on the ancient Greek* experience of democracy, Arendt creates her own concepts to renew political thinking.

### Key Themes

Hannah Arendt organized *The Human Condition* around the theme of the *vita activa*,* a Latin expression meaning "the active life." She identifies three types of active life: labor, work, and action.

Arendt believed that the history of philosophy had not dealt thoroughly enough with all three dimensions of *vita activa*. Instead of differentiating them, philosophers had merged them into a single entity. Arendt attempted to distinguish the three; and perhaps her most important contribution to political theory was in giving more attention to the third element—political action. Arendt attempted to restore a sense of dignity to political action. In her day, as in ours, people too often saw it as an arena in which politicians pursue their own interests rather than serve the public.

Arendt's focus on political action produced three important contributions to the study of politics. First, she moved it away from its fixation with formal rules and institutions. Instead, she focused scholars on what political participants do. In this she differed significantly from

> ❝ With the term *vita activa*, I propose to designate three
> fundamental human activities: labor, work, and action.
> They are fundamental because each corresponds to one
> of the basic conditions under which life on earth has
> been given to man. ❞
>
> Hannah Arendt, *The Human Condition*

behavioralist* social scientists, who were concerned with what might
be analyzed through the observation of human action. Behavioralists
also wanted to move the study of politics away from institutions such
as law-making bodies, but they did so by reducing people to statistics
rather than by trying to understand them.

Second, Arendt offered a full-scale critique of Marxism* and its
focus on economics as the foundation for understanding politics;
according to Marxist thought, history is driven by the struggle
between social classes—a struggle in which economic interests play a
particularly important role.

Finally, in her use of the ancient Greek model of politics, Arendt
proposed an alternative to modern theories of democracy that were
oriented toward consensus and compromise. Instead, she highlighted
the conflict-based ("agonistic")* dimension of democratic politics.
For her, though, this did not require a turn toward violence. Instead,
she envisioned a form of conflict that would continue to keep the
political realm lively and contentious and should lead to the creation
of new and productive forms of political life.

## Exploring the Ideas

For Arendt, "labor" corresponds to people's biological life. Labor
"assures not only individual survival, but the life of the species"[1] by
providing for the biological needs of consumption and reproduction.
Labor remains unceasing, as it creates nothing permanent. Arendt

compares the laborer to the slave: given that the necessities of maintaining life dominate his existence, the laborer cannot be said to be free. Slavery here does not mean being owned by another, but being "owned" by the necessities of life. Those necessities prevent us from being able to see beyond the immediacy of our daily physical needs.

When Arendt speaks of "work," she refers to the fabrication of an artificial world of semi-permanent things not found in nature. A builder, an architect, a craftsman, or artist provides "the human artifact,"[2] a common world of spaces and institutions in which human life takes place. Work differs from labor because it is not bound up with nature and survival. Human projects and creations transform nature, giving rise to objects and institutions recognized around the world. Thus, work carries with it a certain quality of freedom. But it follows an instrumental scheme: individuals are bound by the tasks set for them rather than being free to improvise and act as they wish.

"Action" corresponds to the activity that retains the greatest freedom from necessity. Means and ends come together in the action, which occurs in a public space of appearance, in which agents become visible. Activity appears in the plurality* of the public realm, among and with other people. For example: we may understand demonstrating in the streets as a political action because it makes a cause and principles visible. And it does so whether or not the activism succeeds. So for Arendt action and freedom are synonyms. Both represent the human capacity to create the new and unexpected, elements unconstrained by the rules of cause and effect.

## Language and Expression

Arendt frequently refers to ancient Greek concepts, though she does not simply apply them to the contemporary context. She practices a two-step conceptual analysis: after situating the concepts in their historical and political contexts, she analyzes their transformations and meanings through the course of history.

Some readers may be confused by the absence of a systematic and single argument within the work. Fully understanding Arendt's unique, unorthodox, and complex thinking can require multiple readings. But *The Human Condition*'s plan follows the author's phenomenological\* investigation. As a phenomenological theorist, Arendt approaches conceptual ideas by introducing their commonsense meaning, or what they "appear" to be. But she then alters them, presenting them as they *might* appear in other ways and to other people. She does not seek to develop a "true" definition of the terms under consideration. Instead she looks to create a set of categories that arise from the world of appearances. These categories evolve and develop as she uses them. She presents all the key concepts in the first chapter, and addresses them repeatedly throughout the book. It has been noted that Arendt developed her theoretical framework like an impressionist painter: as she emphasizes some core ideas, she exposes their characteristics with "small brush-strokes."[3]

## NOTES

1   Hannah Arendt, *The Human Condition* (Chicago: University of Chicago Press, 1998), 8.

2   Arendt, *The Human Condition*, 8.

3   Dermot Moran, *Introduction to Phenomenology* (London & New York: Routledge, 2000), 318.

# MODULE 6
# SECONDARY IDEAS

## KEY POINTS

- Arendt formulated the idea of natality*—giving birth to new things through political action.

- Using her idea of political action, she highlighted how practicing forgiveness can reverse a political action, giving it a new political meaning.

- Our ability to act politically to create new realities offers us the potential to deal with environmental problems.

### Other Ideas

In *The Human Condition*, Hannah Arendt introduces a secondary idea that she calls natality. She argues that natality gives action the ability to create something from nothing. Just as giving birth creates a new life, so political action creates something radically new—an institution, idea, or space that had not existed before. Of course, just as with birth, political action is just one part of a narrative. Other processes must precede it. But Arendt proposes that political actions can radically revise and create new things, just as a revolution may create a new social and political landscape, or a political institution might shape political life.

A second idea arising from her emphasis on political action is forgiveness. Critics have not always seen this as a political concept. But Arendt argues that forgiveness holds a unique place in political life because it reverses a previous action, situation, or condition. Unlike promising, an important form of political action that creates a bond between people, forgiveness radically disconnects individuals from

> **❝** All three activities and their corresponding conditions are intimately connected with the most general condition of human existence: birth and death, natality and mortality. **❞**
>
> Hannah Arendt, *The Human Condition*

their previous conditions and actions. It creates something new in the process, but only by destroying something that had existed before. Both forgiving and natality create new realities, but forgiving does so only by reversing a previous action.

### Exploring the Ideas

At one level, Arendt's idea of natality remains a simple one. Giving birth is a fundamental part of human existence. Yet by making political action analogous with it, she breathes new life into the idea, giving it an important resonance it had lacked before. Natality, as a condition of political practice, celebrates the unpredictability of political action. Just as we cannot know how a child will develop, so we cannot know how our political actions will turn out.

This idea of natality also allows Arendt to link action and speech. Arendt argues that no action can take place without some narration to give it meaning. The narrative we construct around our actions reveals not only the action but the one acting. In political action, we create new spaces and ideas and we also recreate, give birth to ourselves. As Arendt puts it: "In acting and speaking, men show who they are, reveal actively their unique personal identities and thus make their appearance in the human world, while their physical identities appear without any activity of their own in the unique shape of the body and sound of the voice."[1] For Arendt, this means that when we narrate our actions, when we describe what we do in public, we create ourselves anew, giving birth over and over again to a new reality.

The other idea that Arendt draws from her conceptual apparatus is forgiveness. Arendt notes that the ancient Greeks,* to whom she turns so much, did not see forgiveness as a political virtue. Instead, she suggests that Jesus of Nazareth* made forgiveness a large part of political life. Arendt suggests that in making forgiveness so prominent, Jesus gave us the means to reverse political action, to sever us from our previous actions, but at the same time to create something new. "The freedom contained in Jesus' teachings of forgiveness is the freedom from vengeance, which encloses both doer and sufferer in the relentless automatism of the action process, which by itself need never come to an end."[2]

## Overlooked

Arendt begins and ends her book with the relationship of humans to the earth. The introduction opens with a reflection on Sputnik,* the Soviet* satellite that was launched into space in 1957, only a year before the book's publication. Arendt noted that this represented the first time a man-made object had been moved into the arena of heavenly bodies. She felt it an important historical occasion. For Arendt, Sputnik's significance had less to do with the political circumstances that informed it than with the urge to leave Earth behind. She wondered whether this would be the first step toward the human race "escaping" the confines of the earth. She concluded by worrying about human alienation from the "world" or from the things, institutions, and spaces that give meaning to our lives. Few have explored Arendt's reflections on how our relationship to the world defines *the human condition*. Her point does not necessarily center on environmentalism, though it might have relevance for thinking about environmental issues. By emphasizing natality and political action, she clearly sees the potential for shaping the world in which we live, perhaps in radical ways, but she always keeps in mind how we are bound by our very human condition and this existence on Earth.

## NOTES

1    Hannah Arendt, *The Human Condition* (Chicago: University of Chicago Press, 1998), 179.

2    Arendt, *The Human Condition*, 241.

# MODULE 7
# ACHIEVEMENT

## KEY POINTS

- Arendt's theory of action and politics successfully challenged the contemplative* philosophical approach and explained its incapacity to really understand *the human condition*.

- In the post-World War II* era, Arendt's account of action and politics as having the potential to create by acting together brought a message of hope.

- Many critics in the years after its publication underlined the book's lack of clarity and conceptual confusions.


### Assessing The Argument

With *The Human Condition*, Hannah Arendt made an important effort to renew thinking around action and politics. Her emphasis on action influenced the development of contemporary political theory. She also intended to challenge the study of politics in the English–speaking world. She believed that political philosophers remained too concerned with Platonic* truths (the idea, drawn from the ancient Greek* philosopher Plato,* that "truth" can be found in the world of ideas), political scientists too concerned with formal institutions, and social scientists too concerned with reducing everything to economic forces. She focused on political action as a human practice in which a people creates and recreates itself. This put her in conflict with a range of different approaches, including idealist* philosophy (a tradition that focuses on the world of ideas as opposed to material reality), behavioralist* political science (a philosophy of social science that emphasizes the importance of analyzing human behavior, drawing

> 66 Hannah Arendt is preeminently the theorist of beginnings. All her books are tales of the unexpected (whether concerned with the novel horrors of totalitarianism or the new dawn of revolution), and reflections on the human capacity to start something new. When she published *The Human Condition* in 1958, she herself sent something unexpected out to the world, and forty years later the book's originality is as striking as ever. 99
>
> Margaret Canovan, introduction to *The Human Condition*

heavily on statistical analysis), and Marxist*-inspired sociology and economics. Also, by using the ancient Greek philosophers to make her point, Arendt challenged assumptions built into modernity (a term used in history, philosophy, art, and politics to describe both a time period—the early twentieth century—and a general approach that focused on the importance of technology and scientific rationality when addressing social and political life).

Many scholars had begun to believe that the modern world defined by technology and progress had rendered historical studies of politics irrelevant. Critics continue to debate how successful Arendt was in reorienting the study of politics. Her work stood against so many different trends that few embraced it directly. Still, the challenge she raised remains important for the study of politics to this day.

## Achievement In Context

Arendt embedded *The Human Condition* in a historical conceptual framework. She intended to provide a new framework that could help people understand the modern world and some of the recent tragic events of the twentieth century. Arendt aimed her new science of politics at a wider audience than just academics. She wanted to provide an alternative to the dominant political context of her day—the tense nuclear standoff between the Soviet Union* and the Union States, and nations aligned to them, that defined the Cold War.* By offering a decisive critique of Marx* and his disciples, she undermined the attraction some in the developing world had developed for the political models of the Soviet Union and Maoist* China (Maoism was the communist* ideology named after the Chinese political leader Mao Zedong, which applied Marxist thought to the largely agricultural society of mid-twentieth-century China).

More, she also undermined the American belief in technology and pragmatism as the solution to political problems, a belief associated with scholars such as American political scientists John Dewey and Louis Hartz. Arendt held an agonistic* democratic perspective (the idea that democracy should be founded on a kind of conflict beneficial to political life): politics is about acting in the public realm and seeking to promote ideas that not only provide radical alternatives but present the self in new ways. This did not sit well with the American pragmatist tradition, which emphasized solving problems by any means necessary. So neither side in the Cold War embraced Arendt's ideas.

## Limitations

While influential in some contexts, the text's unique approach kept it from finding a wider audience. It can be difficult to translate the phenomenological* tradition, with its emphasis on appearance rather than some mystical "reality," into actual political analysis. Indeed, some have suggested that Arendt's idea of political action has no substance. People can "act," but the act itself rather than its outcome remains Arendt's greatest concern. So her ideas may seem unsuitable for studies of politics that seek concrete solutions to actual problems. In addition, her critique of Marx alienated many who draw from that tradition.[1] Even political theorists who might share some of her concerns have been critical of her work. The American political philosopher Sheldon Wolin,* for instance, argued that *The Human Condition* fails to theorize the social dimension of democratic politics adequately.[2]

Arendt did not fit well into any particular political orientation. As a recent German immigrant to the United States, she was just beginning to connect to the American context when she wrote *The Human Condition*. But she refused to attach herself to any particular political orientation, saying she was neither liberal nor conservative.[3] Because of this failure to align herself with a particular political ideology, her practical impact remained limited.

## NOTES

1   See Antonio Negri, *Insurgencies: Constituent Power and the Modern State*, translated by Maurizia Boscagli, foreword by Michael Hardt (Minneapolis: University of Minnesotar Press, 2009).

2   Sheldon Wolin, "Hannah Arendt: Democracy and the Political," *Salmagundi* 60 (Spring–Summer 1983): 3–19.

3   Larry May and Jerome Kohn, eds., *Hannah Arendt: Twenty Years Later* (Boston: MIT Publications, 1996) 1.

# MODULE 8
# PLACE IN THE AUTHOR'S LIFE AND WORK

## KEY POINTS

- *The Human Condition* remains Hannah Arendt's key theoretical work.

- It brought to fruition ideas that she developed in *the Origins of Totalitarianism* and which played out in later political essays and major works, such as *Eichmann in Jerusalem* and *On Revolution*.

- Arendt's unpublished works on a theory of politics also build on *The Human Condition*.

### Positioning

In 1952, six years before she published *The Human Condition*, Hannah Arendt received a grant from the Guggenheim Foundation,* a philanthropic institution, to study Marxism* and totalitarianism.* This allowed her to continue themes she had developed in *The Origins of Totalitarianism* (1951), the work that first made her name as a scholar. In this work, she argues that totalitarianism arises from practices and projects, such as colonialism* (the unequal rule of one country by another), and anti-Semitism* (hatred of and discrimination against Jews), which both denigrate the equality of human beings. She also suggests that nationalism* (a political ideology in which defending the nation is the most important political principle), with its inherent exclusivity, also contributed to the rise of totalitarianism.

Pursuing this research led her to so many issues and questions that she never completed the initial project. But she did develop many

> **❝** I set out to write a little study of Marx, but, but—as soon as one grasps Marx one realizes that one cannot deal with him without taking into account the whole tradition of political philosophy. **❞**
>
> Hannah Arendt, in Elisabeth Young-Bruehl, Hannah *Arendt: For Love Of The World*

ideas from it, such as reflections on the origins and conditions of the *vita activa*\* ("the active life"), which she presented in a series of lectures at Princeton University and the University of Chicago. These lectures, about the different human activities such as labor, work, and action, provided the basis for *The Human Condition*. Her later works deepened this exploration.

Arendt's works helped renew discussions on the nature of political life. "Within the space of four years, from 1958 to 1962, Hannah Arendt released three books, *The Human Condition, Between Past and Future,* and *On Revolution,* all of which had grown from the original Marxism book."[1] In essays compiled under the title *Between Past and Future* (1961), Arendt developed her ideas about political action in relation to authority, freedom, education, and history. And she elaborated on aspects of the theoretical framework she had put forward in *The Human Condition,* making the ideas more concrete. Her next book, *On Revolution* (1963), further developed these ideas in relation to the quintessential mode of political action—revolutionary politics.

## Integration

We may see Arendt's body of work as an ambitious attempt to build a new theory of politics. As she wrote to a friend in 1972, "we all have only one real thought in our lives, and everything we then do are elaborations or variations of one theme."[2] *The Human Condition* represented a pivotal point in her scholarly output, for it laid down the main theoretical elements of her work. She developed these themes in her studies of the philosophical approach of phenomenology.* She refined them as she explored the concrete manifestations of politics in her adopted country, the United States. And of course she continued to reflect on politics in relation to Germany and Israel throughout her career.

Arendt demonstrated her commitment to the practice of politics by pursuing an active political life. Two important controversies exemplify this. The first was her reporting for the *New Yorker* magazine on the trial of Adolph Eichmann,* a former Nazi* bureaucrat who had been kidnapped in Argentina by Israeli special operations forces in 1960. His trial—the first trial of World War II* crimes against humanity to be held in Israel rather than Germany—gained international attention. Eichmann was found guilty and was executed in 1962. Arendt attended the entire trial and published her reports both as magazine articles and eventually as a book, *Eichmann in Jerusalem*.

The book was controversial for two reasons. First, Arendt noted that Jewish agencies in various European countries helped facilitate the movement of Jews to the concentration camps,* making them complicit in the crimes. Jewish groups around the world argued that Arendt was blaming the victim, but in fact she was blaming the bureaucratic nature of political life. This became clearer in the phrase that she coined to describe Eichmann's actions: the "banality of evil." Some believed this detracted from the importance of Eichmann's crimes. But Arendt intended to point out that evil is not always committed in heroic, public ways; sometimes it occurs in secret, in the banal environment of a bureaucratic meeting. This corresponded to an argument she made in *The Human Condition*, which asserted political action as a way of revealing oneself, and castigated modern politics for hiding behind the veneer of bureaucracy.

The second public controversy in which Arendt became embroiled involved desegregation in the United States. Desegregation was the attempt to end the practice of segregation that relegated some individuals to a lesser or separate status, often along racial lines; in this case, the African American population. In 1957, nine black students tried to enroll at the Central High School in the city of Little Rock, Arkansas. But the state's governor blocked their entry. They were only allowed to enroll once the federal government had intervened. Photos of the teenagers being abused by whites objecting to desegregation drove Arendt to write an article for *Commentary* magazine in 1959, in which she criticized the children's parents for subjecting them to this abuse. Many read this as a defense of segregation. But Arendt based her argument on the distinction between the public and private realms— an argument she developed in *The Human Condition*. She believed that without a private realm, in which childhood and education take precedence, we cannot engage in the public realm of political controversy. For her, the Little Rock episode blurred the boundaries between the public and private.

## Significance

*The Human Condition* arguably remains Hannah Arendt's most important book. It had a tremendous impact both inside and outside the academic community, and rewarded Arendt with international recognition. As her biographer, Elisabeth Young-Bruehl,* notes: "During the next twenty-four years, with her many essays and books, from *The Human Condition* to *the Life of the Mind,* Arendt won international fame and a place of pre-eminence among the theorists of her generation."[3] More importantly, *The Human Condition* remains a significant book in the development of Arendt's thought. The text offers an original contribution to philosophical approaches to politics; but we also need to see it in the broader context of her rich intellectual journey.

The theoretical and philosophical focus of *The Human Condition* meant that it did not expand Arendt's reputation far outside the scholarly realm. *The Origins of Totalitarianism* (1951) and *Eichmann in Jerusalem* (1963) won her greater acclaim, probably because they were more directly connected to the events of the day. Yet to understand those books we must first understand the theoretical arguments of *The Human Condition*, arguably her most significant theoretical work even though it may not be her most popular.

## NOTES

1    Elisabeth Young-Bruehl, *Hannah Arendt: For Love Of The World* (New Haven: Yale University Press, 2004), 279.

2    Hannah Arendt, in *Hannah Arendt, For Love Of The World* by Elisabeth Young-Bruehl (New Haven: Yale University Press, 2004), 327.

3    Young-Bruehl, *Hannah Arendt*, ix.

# SECTION 3
## IMPACT

# MODULE 9
# THE FIRST RESPONSES

## KEY POINTS

- Criticisms of *The Human Condition* focused on Arendt's use of other thinkers' work, her conceptual distinctions, and her account of "action."

- Arendt never modified her theoretical or methodological approaches in response to criticism. But she tried to explain her core ideas better in subsequent works.

- The various criticisms of Arendt's work reveal the different aspects of the intellectual, ideological, and political battlefields of that time.

### Criticism

In the years following its 1958 publication, Hannah Arendt's The *Human Condition* attracted much attention and analysis. Critics focused on both the overall work and on specific elements of it. They pointed to three main areas: Arendt's methodological approach, the structure of her argument, and the way she used other thinkers' concepts.

Critics such as the American political philosopher Sheldon Wolin* attacked Arendt's methodology, in particular her references to ancient Greece.* In "Hannah Arendt: Democracy and the Political," he suggested the references to antiquity* were both anachronistic*—that is, they inappropriately projected modern expectations on to ancient times—and elitist.[1] He argued that Arendt failed to appreciate the complexity of Athenian politics, including the importance of the daily economic concerns that motivated some of the political debate.

The Russian British philosopher and political theorist Isaiah Berlin* criticized the text for lacking a structured argument. For him,

 

> 66 While I feel that within the necessary limitations of a historical study and political analysis I made myself sufficiently clear on certain general perplexities which have come to light through the full development of totalitarianism, I also know that I failed to explain the particular method which I came to use, and to account for a rather unusual approach [to] the whole field of political and historical sciences as such. One of the difficulties of the book is that it does not belong to any school and hardly uses any of the officially recognized or officially controversial instruments. 99
>
> Hannah Arendt, "[Origins of Totalitarianism]: A Reply," *The Review of Politics*

Arendt "produces no arguments, no evidence of serious philosophical or historical thought. It is all a stream of metaphysical* free association. She moves from one sentence to another, without logical connection."[2] Crucially, the lack of a single overarching framework made her theory difficult for some to accept. She developed a plurality* of ideas in a complex and unorthodox argument inspired by many philosophers. Scholars often criticized her unique readings of other thinkers and her attempts to synthesize and incorporate their viewpoints into her own position.[3]

Third, the distinctions drawn by Arendt caused controversy. This stemmed primarily from the fact that she collected her concepts from different contexts. For instance, many feminist* theorists—thinkers engaged with the cultural analysis of the struggle for equality between the sexes—have criticized her separation of the "social question" from "political action." The German-born political theorist Hanna Pitkin*[4] confronted Arendt's distinction between private and public and the hierarchy that she placed them in, arguing that this tended to define motherhood and family as belonging to the private sphere and, therefore, lacking freedom. Marxists* also criticized Arendt's exclusion of economic and social issues from the political realm. They argued that doing so took questions of poverty and exploitation out of the political debate and made it impossible to address social injustice. Even some of Arendt's supporters considered this criticism significant.

## Responses

Arendt did not respond directly to criticism. But she did develop her thinking in ways that addressed some of her critics' concerns. In *On Revolution* (1963), she explained how an emphasis on the "social" can lead to further conflict and violence. She did this by comparing the American and French revolutions. In her analysis, the American Revolution* of 1775–81 succeeded because it focused on the political; the French Revolution* of 1789–93 failed because it arose from social concerns such as inequality (although the revolution created a democratic political system, it soon collapsed, leading to the rise of the dictator Napoleon Bonaparte in 1799).

In *Between Past and Future* (1968), Arendt demonstrated how her insights could apply to more concrete situations, such as education and culture. *On Violence* (1970) proposed a radical new theory of power, which further developed the idea of political action already set out in The *Human Condition*. In this work Arendt argues that power does not mean being in a position to dominate others, which she sees as violence. Instead, it represents the coming together of many people to enact change. In the book, she uses this idea to examine the student protests against the Vietnam War* (a Cold War*-era conflict in which the United States engaged with communist* North Vietnam between 1964 and 1973, with the loss of many lives on each side). While she supported these protests, she also criticized the way they sometimes focused on university governance rather than the war.

We may see Arendt's definition of power as a way to clarify the fact that political action does not simply mean a single hero acting alone. It can be a form of cooperative political action that might lead to new insights and institutions.

## Conflict and Consensus

Interest in Arendt has recently increased, as scholars see her work extending into fields such as international relations[5] (the study of interactions between nation states). New efforts are underway to clarify her political concepts.[6] Her published works have been reissued and the Hannah Arendt Center at Bard College in the state of New York has given scholars access to her previously unpublished essays. This has resulted in new insights into her ideas.[7] Scholars currently agree that she played a crucial role in presenting alternatives to dominant modes of political analysis. Yet while her work has become more influential, we cannot say that political scientists or scholars have actually embraced it. Her unique approach to politics encourages readers to engage with her critically, rather than simply accept her ideas.

The *Human Condition* is, effectively, Arendt's attempt to conceptualize the implications of alienation from the world. If we must take action to renew the world, we must do so by connecting citizens back to one another and to an idea of a common world or a common life. Arendt felt the modern world had eroded this sense of commonality, and she was attempting to develop the theoretical foundation to restore it—so that, in turn, we can overcome the alienation of the world. This is why her idea of political action endures, more than half a century after she raised it.

# NOTES

1    Sheldon Wolin, "Hannah Arendt: Democracy and the Political," *Salmagundi* 60 (Spring–Summer 1983): 3–19.

2    Ramin Jahanbegloo, *Conversations with Isaiah Berlin* (London: Peter Alban, 1992), 82.

3    For an overview of various criticisms, see Walter Laqueur, "The Arendt Cult: Hannah Arendt as Political Commentator," *Journal of Contemporary History* 33, no. 4 (1998): 483–96.

4    Hanna Pitkin, "Justice: On Relating Private and Public," *Political Theory* 9, no. 3 (1981): 327–52.

5    Anthony F. Lang, Jr. and John Wlliams, eds., *Hannah Arendt and International Relations: Reading Across the Lines* (New York: Palgrave, 2005).

6    Patrick Hayden, ed., *Hannah Arendt: Key Concepts* (New York: Routledge, 2014).

7    For instance, Hannah Arendt, *Responsibility and Judgment*, edited by Jerome Kohn (New York: Shocken Books, 2005); Hannah Arendt, *The Promise of Politics*, edited by Jerome Kohn (New York: Schocken Books, 2007); Hannah Arendt, *Essays in Understanding, 1930-1954* (New York: Schocken Books, 2005); and Hannah Arendt, *The Jewish Writings*, edited by Jerome Kohn (New York: Schocken Books, 2008).

# MODULE 10
## THE EVOLVING DEBATE

## KEY POINTS

- The concept of natality* (the potential for political action to create new institutions and realities) can be usefully transferred to the creative arts.

- Although Arendt never founded a school of thought around her work, a large community of independent thinkers have used and discussed her theoretical framework.

- Many scholars from various disciplines have drawn on Arendt's work, most famously the German philosopher Jürgen Habermas.* This underlines the importance of her material.

### Uses And Problems

The ideas Hannah Arendt explores in *The Human Condition* have been taken up in many different fields. The Scottish educator Morwenna Griffiths* has noted how Arendt's notion of natality can be useful in the arts.[1] Arendt's model of human affairs relies on change: every time new human beings come into the world and develop to the point of acting in it, the model changes. Arendt emphasizes natality over mortality in human experience, encouraging us to think of ourselves as beings who are first and foremost *born*. The fact of being born gives every human a unique life story that, in turn, makes each person unique. But Arendt develops this idea to suggest that we only acquire our unique life story to the extent that we *act* within the world, and disclose ourselves to the world and to others. All actions have consequences and we respond to those consequences by engaging in more actions.

> ❝ Each time you write something you send it to the world and it becomes public, obviously everybody is free to do with it what he pleases, and this is as it should be. ❞
>
> Hannah Arendt, "Remarks to the American Society of Christian Ethics"

This full sequence of actions and consequences comprises the story of any one person's life and creativity. The ability to be defined by the possibility of creating something new, to be constantly beginning rather than ending, has special significance for creative artists. Artists are, in a sense, fabricators with a capacity for originality. In Arendt's terms, they are actors requiring spectators—their action needs to take place in the public realm. In this way, action and artistry have a close connection to the condition of natality: the new beginning inherent in birth can make itself felt in the world only through the capacity for constantly creating something new.

## Schools of Thought

Although Arendt's work developed a great following, she never tried to create a unified school of thought around her work during her lifetime. Two related but slightly divergent schools of thought have nevertheless formed around *The Human Condition*. The first approach, deliberative democratic theory,* has been spearheaded by the Turkish American political philosopher Selya Benhabib*[2] and the German philosopher Jürgen Habermas.[3] Habermas used Arendt's distinction of *praxis** (action) versus *poiesis* (making) to differentiate the concept of work from what he calls "communicative action." For Habermas, "Hannah Arendt's principal philosophical work, *The Human Condition* (1958), serves to systematically renew the Aristotelian* concept of *praxis*."[4]

The second group of theorists who have used Arendt's work are agonistic* democrats (those who hold the position that democracy is founded on a degree of conflict), who include the feminist* theorist Bonnie Honig[5] and the political scientist Patchen Markell,[6] both Americans. Their works focus on the importance of creating spaces for politics, but they emphasize the conflicts inherent in the nature of political interactions. For them, disagreement remains a crucial part of democracy.

## In Current Scholarship

*The Human Condition* has influenced many contemporary scholars. The two schools of democratic theories mentioned above may be the most prominent, but Arendt has also influenced other contemporary theorists from different disciplines. For instance, the idea of narrative as an important part of social and political theory influenced the work of the New Zealand-born anthropologist Michael D. Jackson.* Jackson used Arendt's work on storytelling to explore cross-cultural issues.[7]

In international relations, Arendt has been an important influence on contemporary scholars such as Patrick Hayden,* Anthony F. Lang Jr.,* Patricia Owens, and John Williams; scholars who draw on her work as a resource to counter the emphasis on global anarchy. In her works they find the potential for seeing global politics in new ways. In particular, Arendt's ideas have helped reinterpret debates about the use of force, war crimes, and global governance. Legal scholars have returned to her work, studying her ideas about legislation (law-making) and constitutional theory (theory about a nation's obligations and nature, as defined by law). These scholars have argued that she can be read as a theorist of law-making and not just of political action, especially in regard to narrating the political conditions that create the law.[0]

# NOTES

1   See Morwenna Griffiths, "Research and the Self," in *The Routledge Companion to Research in the Arts*, eds. Michael Biggs and Henrik Karlsson (Oxford: Routledge, 2011), 168.

2   Selya Benhabib, *The Reluctant Modernism of Hannah Arendt* (Thousand Oaks, CA: Sage Publishers, 1996) and Selya Benhabib, ed., *Politics in Dark Times: Encounters with Hannah Arendt* (New York: Cambridge University Press, 2010).

3   Jürgen Habermas, "Hannah Arendt's Communications Concept of Power," *Social Research* 44, no. 1(Spring 1977): 5.

4   Habermas, "Hannah Arendt's Communications Concept of Power," 5.

5   Bonnie Honig, *Political Theory and the Displacement of Politics* (Ithaca, NY: Cornell University Press, 1993) and Bonnie Honig, ed., *Feminist Interpretations of Hannah Arendt* (University Park, PA: Penn State University Press, 1995).

6   Patchen Markell, "The Rule of the People: Arendt, *Arche*, and Democracy," *American Political Science Review* 100, no. 1 (2006): 1–14.

7   Michael D. Jackson, *The Politics of Storytelling: Violence, Transgression and Intersubjectivity* (Copenhagen: Museum Tuscalanum Press, 2002).

8   Christian Volk, *Arendtian Constitutionalism: Law, Politics and the Order of Freedom* (Oxford: Hart Publishers, 2015).

# IMPACT AND INFLUENCE TODAY

## KEY POINTS

- *The Human Condition* explains why political protest continues to erupt and why such protests often fail to create new institutions.

- *The Human Condition*'s framework still challenges classical analysis by underlining the unpredictability of *the human condition*. Moreover, Arendt's conceptual distinctions question conventional ways of analyzing reality.

- Many discussions and criticisms—mainly about Arendt's theoretical distinctions—have enriched the ways in which scholars see the text in its original context.

## Position

More than half a century after its publication, Hannah Arendt's *The Human Condition* continues to contribute to ongoing debates in political theory and political life. In 2000, *a Cambridge Companion* to Arendt—a volume discussing her ideas and work—was published, indicating the importance of her thought across a wide range of disciplines and approaches.[1] Her ideas have become influential in fields as diverse as international relations[2] and legal theory.[3] Throughout all these writings, the ideas introduced in *The Human Condition* remain central.

The basic question that Arendt asked in *The Human Condition* remains relevant to contemporary political debates. She challenges existing mind-sets by differentiating the social sphere from the political. On the basis of this distinction, she develops new ways of thinking about freedom and political action. Her ideas have great

> 66 Much as Arendt herself appropriated the political tradition of the West, not in the spirit of a scholastic exercise, but in the spirit of questioning and dialogue such as to orient the mind in the present, we too can engage with her work today to illuminate some of the deepest political perplexities of our times. One of these perplexities is the changing boundaries of the political in our societies, and with it the shifting line between the public and private realms. 99
>
> Seyla Benhabib, "Feminist Theory and Hannah Arendt's Concept of Public Space," *History of the Human Sciences*

relevance in the current world order, especially as protests have erupted around the world in response to neoliberal* economic structures (economic structures in which government intervention in the markets is discouraged, and privatization encouraged). For instance, the worldwide Occupy Movements* (anti-capitalist action groups that have sprung up since the financial crisis of 2008), might well find Arendt's thinking helpful, being typical instances of political action. If these grassroots actions have failed to develop concrete alternatives, this might be because they focus excessively on the "social" rather than on the politics of creating new institutions.

### Interaction

Arendt wrote about the way in which the rise of the social threatens the political. These ideas remain relevant today (when, for example, politicians inappropriately compare managing national debt to a family managing its household debt). But politics is much more than this. In Arendt's view, it should be about creating democratic spaces in which equality and freedom can flourish. Her theory of the social eating away at politics, which suggests a harsh criticism of consumer society, stands at odds with the theories of both liberal\* and Marxist\*-oriented scholars. Most political debate revolves around social policy, and tends to avoid explicitly political themes. Although British political parties, for example, continue to invoke the need for a constitutional convention (a meeting during which representatives of a people come together to draft a constitution) they have not convened one—perhaps because they remain more focused on pleasing constituencies with new policy initiatives than on facing the hard work of creating new institutions and ideas.

The Scottish Referendum\* of 2014 (a vote taken on Scottish independence from the United Kingdom), one radical effort to confront the distinctly political question of sovereignty, generated much political dialogue in Scotland. The discussion suggested that Arendt had a point. People do not simply want social policies that deal with their daily lives; they want to engage in serious debate about political institutions and ideas. By insisting that the private and public, the social and political should be separated, Arendt remained unable to analyze the conflicts that arise when defining the boundaries between them. If this distinction between labor and action made her "unpopular with many on the left, her account of action brought a message of hope and encouragement to other radicals, including some in the Civil Rights movement\* and behind the Iron Curtain"[4] ("the Civil Rights movement" refers to a number of related social movements in the US demanding equality for African Americans; "the Iron Curtain" was the name for the border between communist\* Eastern Europe and the democratic West between 1945 and 1989).

## The Continuing Debate

Many thinkers have criticized Arendt's private/public and social/political distinctions for being too rigid. Feminist\* scholars such as Hanna Pitkin\* castigated *The Human Condition* for neglecting the issue of gender—a typical concern for feminist scholars, whose reading and analysis of culture focuses on the various implications of inequality between men and women. As the Turkish American philosopher Selya Benhabib* says: "For contemporary feminist theory Hannah Arendt's thought remains puzzling, challenging and, at times, infuriating."[5] But Arendt's stance on gender remained more complicated than it first appeared. She defined labor as the activity dedicated to sustaining human life. Labor also provides for the biological needs of consumption and reproduction. These activities take place in the private realm of the household and are characterized by their necessity, so the person performing them lacks freedom. In this way, Arendt tacitly linked motherhood to notions of labor and, consequently, potential enslavement. Still, for her, natality* (birth) also represented new beginnings characteristic of freedom and political action.

Another example of critical discussion of Arendt's theory comes from the sociologist Richard Sennett,* who also challenged her approach to labor. In *The Human Condition*, Arendt classified *animal laborans* (Latin for a laborer) as inferior to *homo faber* (Latin for worker/ maker). In his book *The Craftsman*, Sennett criticizes this division of practical life, arguing that the craftsman's activity goes far beyond skilled manual labor.

## NOTES

1   Dana Villa, ed., *The Cambridge Companion to Hannah Arendt* (Cambridge: Cambridge University Press, 2000).

2   Anthony F. Lang, Jr. and John Williams, eds., *Hannah Arendt and International Relations: Reading Across the Lines* (London: Palgrave, 2006); Patricia Owens, *Between War and Politics: International Relations and the Thought of Hannah Arendt* (Oxford: Oxford University Press, 2008); and Patrick Hayden, *Political Evil in a Global Age: Hannah Arendt and International Theory* (London: Routledge, 2009).

3   Marco Goldini and Christopher McCorkindale, eds., *Hannah Arendt and the Law* (Oxford: Hart Publishing, 2012).

4    Margaret Canovan, introduction to *The Human Condition* by Hannah Arendt (Chicago: University of Chicago Press, 1998), xv.

5    Seyla Benhabib, "Feminist theory and Hannah Arendt's Concept of Public Space," *History of the Human Sciences* 6 (1993): 97.

# MODULE 12
# WHERE NEXT?

## KEY POINTS

- *The Human Condition* gives us new insights into why political protests persist and what makes them successful.

- The originality and efficiency of Arendt's concepts allow many thinkers to use her theoretical framework in their own projects.

- With *The Human Condition*, Arendt elaborated a unique and unorthodox theoretical framework, which permanently challenged the ideas by which we analyze and understand our political world.

## Potential

Today, what Hannah Arendt herself stood for is as important as the particular ideas set out in *The Human Condition*. She argued that "new beginnings cannot be ruled out even when society seems locked in stagnation or set on an inexorable course."[1] This emphasis on new beginnings has the potential to give meaning to protest movements. Indeed, it holds the key to their success. For Arendt, a protest movement represents the essence of political action—but it will fail if it focuses solely on "social" matters such as poverty or inequality. She understood that protest must begin with such matters, but she believed that, to achieve any concrete results, the protesters need to channel their energy into creating new institutions to address those problems. Arendt can offer insights into how we might create new political institutions to deal with the problems of our day.

Arendt's observations on the unpredictability of politics and her message of hope is likely to be developed further. For instance, her

> ❝ As we stand at the threshold of a new millennium, the one safe prediction we can make is that, despite the continuation of processes already in motion, the open future will become an arena for countless human initiatives that are beyond our present imagination. ❞
>
> Margaret Canovan, introduction to *The Human Condition*

writings on Zionism*—the political movement to build a Jewish nation in the Middle East—of over half a century ago eerily describe the dangers that the world now faces. But she does not offer a simple call to action. For Arendt no human can take action for everybody; human beings in her perspective are plural. We live our lives as unique and very different individuals. Underlining the importance of creation, she states that hope comes from the continuous process of new people being born into this world, each capable of new initiatives.

## Future Directions

Arendt's ideas may help us understand contemporary protest movements such as those that began in the Middle East in 2010 and have come to be called the Arab Spring,* or the Green Revolution* of 2009 following the controversial presidential elections in Iran. In these protests, people were reacting against the kind of rigid bureaucratic structures seen by Arendt as so detrimental to political life. In 2011, Egyptians created a new political system through their protests in Cairo's Tahrir Square. This new system focused only on order and practices of governance; it did not fundamentally change the Egyptian political system, so it failed. We may read this as reflecting Arendt's idea that political action can never be permanent, but must always be renewed. Her revolutionary understanding of political action makes personal projects subordinate to the more significant shared public realm. This both challenges and contributes to our understanding of contemporary politics. Arendt warns about "alienation from the earth"—namely, when "the human capacity to start new things calls all natural limits into question." She also cautions against "alienation from the world," when "automated societies engrossed by ever more efficient production and consumption encourage us to behave and think of ourselves simply as an animal species governed by natural laws."[2] Current scientific and social debates about DNA (the means by which genetic information is passed down the generations), atomic energy, and climate change demonstrate the timeliness of her concerns.

## Summary

In her book on Arendt, Elisabeth Young-Bruehl states Arendt's principal question to be: "How shall we take political events, the political realm, seriously? The terms are simple, but the question is not."[3] A highly original work, *The Human Condition* renewed the debate about politics and philosophy with three key shifts of perspective: first, that action remains a fundamentally political activity of creation and freedom. Second, the corresponding understanding that action has potential power. And third, that there are conceptual distinctions between public and private, and between labor, work, and action. These three elements have changed the traditional analysis of politics, and imply an inversion of its scope. No longer limited to government or institutions, Arendt opens politics to the potential for action, for initiative in the public realm by unique human beings. For Arendt, general philosophical principles cannot regulate the political domain—and that itself raises philosophical questions. Her originality stands out in her fresh view of already familiar concepts. She transcends conventional analysis by proposing a unique and unorthodox approach that has permanently challenged the terms by which we analyze and understand our political world.

## NOTES

1   Margaret Canovan, introduction to *The Human Condition* by Hannah Arendt (Chicago: University of Chicago Press, 1998), xvii.

2   Canovan, introduction to *The Human Condition*, x–xi.

3   Elisabeth Young-Bruehl, *Hannah Arendt: For Love Of The World* (New Haven: Yale University Press, 2004), 322.

# GLOSSARY

# GLOSSARY OF TERMS

**Agonism:** a term in political theory used to describe democracy that highlights disagreement and debate rather than consensus. This disagreement, however, is not violent and can actually benefit political life.

**American Revolution:** the revolution undertaken by American colonists in 1775 against the British government, which lasted until 1781, when the 13 American colonies created a single United States of America.

**Anachronistic:** a contemporary definition of a historical term or idea that fails to account for the differences between time periods. For example, it would be anachronistic to say that "democracy" is something that applied to ancient Athens in the same way that it does to contemporary Britain.

**Analytic Philosophy:** an approach to philosophy, largely found in Anglo-American universities, that focuses mainly on logic and meaning rather than metaphysical questions.

**Ancient Greece:** the period of Greek civilization that lasted from the eighth to the sixth centuries B.C.E.

**Antiquity:** generally used to refer to "classical" ancient civilizations prior to the Middle Ages, especially those of Greece and Rome.

**Anti-Semitism:** hostility, discrimination, prejudice, or hatred toward Jews.

**Arab Spring:** a term used to describe a series of violent and nonviolent protests, demonstrations, and civil wars that swept through the Arab world in 2010.

**Aristotelian:** philosophical approaches that draw on the ideas of the ancient Greek philosopher Aristotle (384 B.C.E.–322 B.C.E.)

**Behaviouralism:** a philosophy of social science that emphasizes the importance of analyzing human behavior rather than looking at formal institutions or ideas. Its methods draw heavily on statistical and quantitative analysis.

**Capitalism:** an economic system based on private ownership, private enterprise, and the maximization of profit.

**Civil disobedience:** an action, usually peaceful, taken to protest against a government, in which the protester accepts that he or she will be penalized by that government.

**Civil Rights movement:** refers to a number of related social movements in the US demanding equality for African Americans.

**Cold War:** a period of tension between the West and communist countries of the Eastern bloc, which lasted from the late 1940s (after World War II) to the start of the 1990s (with the fall of the Berlin Wall).

**Colonialism:** refers to the rule of one country by another, involving unequal power relations between the ruler (colonist) and ruled (colony), and the exploitation of the colonies' resources to strengthen the economy of the colonizers' home country.

**Communism:** the last stage of Marxist theory, characterized by public ownership of property and natural resources, and of the means of production of goods and services.

**Concentration Camps/Death Camps:** camps created by the Nazi government in World War II that housed Jews, homosexuals, dissidents, and others deemed undesirable. Some camps were designed for work purposes, but most were designed for large-scale, mechanized slaughter of their inmates, usually in gas chambers.

*Conditio per quam:* a Latin phrase meaning "a condition that is sufficient."

*Conditio sine qua non:* a Latin phrase meaning "a condition that is absolutely necessary" (literally, a condition without which something cannot be).

**Contemplative philosophy:** a philosophical approach that emphasizes thought and reflection over action.

**Continental philosophy:** a school of philosophy found largely in France and Germany that draws on historical resources and seeks to explore broad metaphysical questions.

**Contingency:** the idea that we cannot predict the outcome of any course of action.

**Decolonization:** the process whereby nations gain independence from former colonial powers.

**Deliberative democratic theory:** the idea that deliberation (discussion) is an essential element of decision-making for a law to be truly democratic, and that voting alone is not enough,

**Empirical:** relating to something that can be verified by observation.

**Existentialism:** a philosophical approach that emphasizes the lack of any governing order to the universe or reality, associated with twentieth-century French philosophers such as Albert Camus and Jean-Paul Sartre.

**Feminism:** a school of thought based on analysis of society according to gender; it generally aims to institute equality for men and women in the spheres of culture, politics, and the economy.

**French Revolution:** a revolution undertaken by a wide range of groups in France, which began in 1789 and lasted until the execution of the French King Louis XVI in 1793. It created a radically egalitarian society for a period, until Napoleon Bonaparte came to power in 1804.

**Fundamentalist:** a term derived from nineteenth-century Christian theology to describe a belief system that seeks to return to the "fundamentals" or most important elements of a religious tradition. This usually means a literal reading of the religious text in question. It is now used to describe any believer who adopts a literal reading of their religious text and a conservative approach to their religion.

**Green Revolution:** the name for protests that followed presidential elections in Iran in 2009, against the reelection of the incumbent president Mahmoud Ahmadinejad.

**Guggenheim Foundation:** an American philanthropic foundation that funds research in the social sciences and humanities.

**Hegelian:** philosophical approaches that draw on the ideas of the philosopher Georg H.W. Hegel (1770–1831). These approaches usually adopt Hegel's idealist philosophical approach and focus on how ideas determine our reality.

**Hungarian Revolution (1956):** a spontaneous revolt against the Hungarian government. The government used Soviet tanks to repress the protests.

**Idealist:** in philosophy, a tradition that focuses on the world of ideas as opposed to material reality.

**Imperialist:** a term describing foreign policies that seek to create colonies or ensure the dominance of one state over many others. Imperialist can refer to formal empires, such as the Roman Empire, or more informal ones, such as that of the United States today.

**Iron Curtain:** the name commonly used to describe the border between communist Eastern Europe and the democratic West between 1945 and 1989.

**Liberalism:** a current of thought that advocates the freedom of the individual and nonviolent change of political, social, or economic institutions.

**Liberal pluralism:** the belief in liberal political theory, and that a society should accept all forms of moral and religious belief, assuming that those beliefs do not harm others.

**Maoism:** communist ideology named after Mao Zedong, which applied Marxist thought to the largely agrarian society of mid-twentieth-century China. Mao led China through a revolutionary period in the 1940s, then became the Chinese leader from 1949 until his death in 1976.

**Marxism:** a set of political and economic theories developed by the political philosopher Karl Marx and the social scientist Friedrich Engels in the mid-to-late nineteenth century. Marxist theory explains social change in terms of economics and also predicts a proletarian revolution to overthrow capitalism.

**Metaphysics:** in philosophy, metaphysics examines the way things are in the most fundamental way possible.

**Natality:** Hannah Arendt's term to describe the potential held by all political actions for creating new institutions and realities. This potential also leads to unexpected realities; just as no one can predict what a child will become, no one can predict what political actions will produce.

**Nationalism:** a political ideology in which defending the nation is the most important political principle. This reflects a belief that humans benefit from the culture, society, and politics of their particular nation more than from any universal standards or international institutions.

**Nazism:** the ideology of the Nazi Party, which ruled Germany from 1933 to 1945. It is a variety of fascism that involves racism, anti-Semitism, nationalism, and national expansion.

**Neoliberalism:** a more recent version of liberalism (especially in the 1980s and 1990s), neoliberalism is a political position that advocates freedom of the individual and minimal government intervention in economic and social life.

**Objectivism:** in philosophy, a theory stating that reality exists freely or independently from human minds.

**Occupy Movements:** anti-capitalist action groups that have sprung up since the financial crisis of 2008.

**Phenomenology:** in philosophy, a philosophical study of the structures of subjective experience and consciousness. The German philosopher Edmund Husserl* (1859–1938) founded this school of thought.

**Platonic truth:** the idea drawn from the ancient Greek philosopher Plato that "truth" can be found in the world of ideas. Plato's theory is based on the notion that there are ideal forms of everything, which help us to define the objects, institutions, and practices of our real lives.

**Pluralism:** the idea that there are a multiplicity of ways of being in the world, all of which should be respected. This differs from tolerance, which assumes that we should simply accept other views. A pluralist approach claims we can benefit from these alternative views and ideas.

**Positivism:** in philosophy, a theory that confines itself to what can be known via empirical data, scientific methods, and objectivism.

***Praxis/poiesis.*** *praxis* was the ancient Greek term for action. For Arendt, it represented the most important level of the active life. She used Aristotle's distinction between action (*praxis*) and fabrication, or making (*poiesis*) to underline the specifics of the concept of action in her theoretical framework.

**Resistance:** a term used to describe both violent and nonviolent forms of resistance to Nazi occupation, particularly in France during World War II.

**Scottish Referendum (2014):** a vote taken on Scotland's independence from the United Kingdom, in which the Scottish electorate voted to stay within the UK.

**Secular:** a term used to describe a political system or society that is not religious in any way.

**Social democrat:** A political position that combines liberal democracy with a socialist tendency toward redistribution of wealth.

**Soviet Union:** a union of socialist states on the Eurasian continent that existed between 1922 and 1991. It was dissolved in 1991, following revolutions that overthrew Soviet rule in many Central and Eastern European countries.

**Sputnik:** a Soviet satellite launched on October 4, 1957. It was the first satellite to orbit the earth.

**Stalinism:** an ideology conceived and implemented by Joseph Stalin in the Soviet Union from 1929 to 1953, considered a branch of Marxist–Leninist ideology.

**Totalitarianism:** a political system in which the centralized government holds total authority over society, controls private and public life, and requires complete subservience.

**Transcendental:** a term used to describe a reality that is beyond the observable or empirically verifiable. It is often used to describe religious experiences in which individuals feel a connection to the divine.

**Vietnam War (1961–75):** A conflict between the United States and North Vietnam in which the United States sought to protect its nominal ally, South Vietnam. The war was part of the wider Cold War effort to stop the spread of communism. It generated a great deal of opposition in the United States and is considered one of the few wars the US has lost.

*Vita activa / vita contemplativa:* *Vita activa* refers to a life dedicated to action. Its opposite is *vita contemplativa*, meaning a life dedicated to contemplation and thinking. For Arendt, *vita activa* corresponds more to the human condition, although thinkers have traditionally valued the contemplative life more highly.

**World War II (1939–45):** a global conflict fought between the Axis Powers (Germany, Italy, and Japan) and the victorious Allied Powers (the United Kingdom and its colonies, the Soviet Union, and the United States).

**Zionism:** a nationalist and political movement that sees the land of Israel as the rightful homeland of the Jewish people.

# PEOPLE MENTIONED IN THE TEXT

**Aristotle (384 B.C.E.–322 B.C.E.)** was a Greek philosopher and a student of Plato. He is considered a founder of Western philosophy. His writings cover many subjects including physics, biology, logic, ethics, aesthetics, poetry, theater, music, and politics.

**Augustine of Hippo (354–430)** was a North African Christian theologian and philosopher. In his famous work *The City of God*, Augustine sought to reconcile the existence of the Roman Empire with Christian belief, emphasizing the importance of political order for spiritual life.

**Seyla Benhabib (b. 1950)** is a political philosopher at Yale University who specializes in Arendt and Habermas. She is known for combining critical and feminist theory. Her major work on Arendt is *The Reluctant Modernism of Hannah Arendt* (1996).

**Isaiah Berlin (1909–97)** taught at Oxford and was a philosopher, social and political theorist, essayist, and historian of ideas. He is known for his defense of liberalism, and his attacks on political extremism and intellectual fanaticism. His most famous work was *Two Concepts of Liberty* (1958).

**Heinrich Blücher (1899–1970)** was a German poet and philosopher. An anti-Stalinist communist, Blücher encouraged his wife Hannah Arendt to engage with the theories of Marxism.

**Margaret Canovan (b. 1939)** is an English political theorist who specializes in Hannah Arendt. She teaches political thought at the University of Keele. Her major work on Arendt is *Hannah Arendt: A Reinterpretation of Her Political Thought* (1994).

**Bernard Crick (1928–2008)** was a British political scientist. He was concerned with public ethics and politics.

**David Easton (1917–2014)** was a Canadian political scientist who spent most of his life teaching in the United States; he promoted behavioralism as the most important way to study politics.

**Adolf Eichmann (1906–62)** was a Nazi bureaucrat responsible for organizing transport of the Jews of Europe to concentration camps. After escaping to Argentina following the end of World War II, he was captured by the Israelis, put on trial, and executed.

**John Kenneth Galbraith (1908–2006)** was a Canadian economist and diplomat. He was a staunch proponent of liberalism.

**Morwenna Griffiths (b. 1948)** is a professor of education at Edinburgh University who writes on philosophy and education.

**Jürgen Habermas (b. 1929)** is a highly influential German philosopher and sociologist. Over his lifetime he has made major contributions to studies of social and political theory, epistemology, and pragmatism. One of his main works is *The Theory of Communicative Action* (1981).

**Patrick Hayden (b. 1965)** is an international political theorist teaching at the University of St Andrews.

**Georg H. W. Hegel (1770–1831)** was a Prussian philosopher who argued that the world of ideas determines our reality. He introduced the idea of the dialectic, or the process by which opposing ideas interact to create our modern reality. He influenced the work of Karl Marx and many other philosophers.

**Martin Heidegger (1889–1976)** was an influential German philosopher who mainly worked on phenomenology and existentialism, exploring the question of being. Scholars consider Heidegger's *Being and Time*, originally published in 1927, one of the most important philosophical works of the twentieth century. He was romantically involved with Hannah Arendt until the rise of the Third Reich.

**Edmund Husserl (1859–1938)** played an important role in the foundation of the philosophical school of phenomenology, which looks at structures of the subjective experience and consciousness. His masterwork is *Logical Investigations* (1900–1).

**Michael D. Jackson (b. 1940)** is a New Zealand-born poet and anthropologist, and founder of existential anthropology. One of his major works is *The Politics of Storytelling* (2002).

**Karl Jaspers (1883–1969)** was a German philosopher whose work influenced modern theology, psychiatry, and philosophy. One of his major works is *Philosophy* (1932).

**Jesus of Nazareth (c. 4 B.C.E.–30 C.E.)** was a Jewish prophet who lived in Roman Palestine and was the founder of the Christian religion.

**Immanuel Kant (1724–1804)** was a German Enlightenment philosopher who aimed at uniting reason with experience; his major work is *Critique of Pure Reason* (1781).

**Anthony F. Lang, Jr. (b. 1968)** is an international political theorist who teaches at the University of St. Andrews.

**Karl Marx (1818–83)** was a German philosopher and revolutionary socialist. In his most significant work *The Communist Manifesto* (1848), written with Friedrich Engels, he developed the political and economic theories that came to be known as Marxism. Central to Marxist theory is an explanation of social change in terms of economics, along with a prediction that proletariat revolution will overthrow capitalism.

**Charles Merriam (1874–1953)** was an American political scientist who spent much of his career at the University of Chicago. He was a proponent of behavioralism and sought to promote pragmatic solutions to political problems in the US.

**Hanna Pitkin (b. 1931)** is a professor of political science at the University of California, Berkeley. She is known for her reflection on representation, *The Concept of Representation* (1967), and also *The Attack of the Blob: Hannah Arendt's Concept of the Social* (1998).

**Plato (c. 428/7 B.C.E.–348/7 B.C.E.)** was a classical Greek philosopher and founder of the Academy in Athens, who laid the foundations of Western philosophy along with Socrates and Aristotle.

**Karl Popper (1902–94)** was an Austrian British philosopher. He is one of the best-known philosophers of science of the twentieth century.

**John Rawls (1921–2002)** was an American moral and political philosopher. His Theory of Justice (1971) developed an approach that saw justice as fairness, answering to the demands of both freedom and equality of citizens in liberal democracies.

**W. W. Rostow (1916–2003)** was an American political theorist and economist. He was known for his conservative views, including his opposition to communism, and support of capitalism and the Vietnam War.

**Richard Sennett (b. 1943)** is a sociologist at the London School of Economics and New York University who studies social ties in cities, and the effects of urban living on individuals. One of his main works is *The Craftsman* (2008).

**Ludwig Wittgenstein (1889–1951)** was an Austrian-born philosopher who worked mainly in England. His posthumously published masterwork *Philosophical Investigations* (1953) was collated and translated from German to English by his star student Elizabeth Anscombe. This work had an enormous influence on British twentieth-century philosophy.

**Sheldon Wolin (1922–2015)** was an American political theorist whose most famous book, *Politics and Vision*, argued for an approach to politics that avoids grand visions and focuses on democratic practices.

**Elisabeth Young-Bruehl (1946–2011)** was an American academic and psychotherapist who specialized in Arendt. Her most famous work on Arendt was *Hannah Arendt: For Love Of The World* (2004).

# WORKS CITED

# WORKS CITED

Arendt, Hannah. *Between Past and Future: Six Exercises in Political Thought.* New York: Viking, 1961.

*Correspondence with the Rockefeller Foundation.* Washington: Library of Congress, MSS Box, p.013872 (ix).

*Eichmann in Jerusalem: A Report on the Banality of Evil.* New York: Viking Press, 1963.

*The Human Condition.* Introduction by Margaret Canovan. Chicago: The University of Chicago Press, 1998.

*Life of the Mind.* Edited by Mary McCarthy. New York: Harcourt Brace Jovanovich (unfinished on her death), 1978.

*On Revolution.* New York: Viking Press, 1963.

*The Origins of Totalitarianism.* New York: Schocken Books, 2004.

*[The Origins of Totalitarianism]:* "A Reply." *The Review of Politics* 15, no. 1 (1953): 76–84.

*"Reflections on Little Rock."* Dissent 6, no. 1 (Winter 1959): 45–56.

Aristotle. *Nicomachean Ethics.* Translated by Martin Ostwald. New York: Macmillan, 1962.

Barber, Benjamin. *Strong Democracy: Participatory Politics for a New Age.* Berkeley: University of California Press, 1984.

Benhabib, Seyla. "Feminist Theory and Hannah Arendt's Concept of Public Space." *History of the Human Sciences* 6, no. 2 (1993): 97–114.

*The Reluctant Modernism of Hannah Arendt.* New York; Thousand Oaks: Sage, 1996.

Calhoun, Craig, and John McGowan, eds. *Hannah Arendt and the Meaning of Politics.* Minneapolis: University of Minnesota Press, 1997.

Canovan, Margaret. *Hannah Arendt: A Reinterpretation of Her Political Thought.* Cambridge: Cambridge University Press, 1994.

Griffiths, Morwenna. "Research and the Self." In *The Routledge Companion to Research in the Arts.* Edited by Michael Biggs and Henrik Karlsson, 167–185. Oxford: Routledge, 2011.

Habermas, Jürgen. "Hannah Arendt's Communications Concept of Power." Social Research 44, no. 1 (Spring 1977): 3–24.

*The Theory of Communicative Action, Volume 1: Reason and the Rationalization of Society.* Boston: Beacon Press, 1981.

*The Theory of Communicative Action, Volume 2: Lifeworld and System: The Critique of Functionalist Reason.* Boston: Beacon Press, 1981.

*The Structural Transformation of the Public Sphere: An Inquiry into a Category of Bourgeois Society.* Cambridge: Polity, 1989.

Heidegger, Martin. *Being and Time.* New York: Harper & Row, 1962.

Husserl, Edmund. *Logical Investigations.* London: Taylor & Francis, 1970.

Jackson, Michael D. *The Politics of Storytelling: Violence, Transgression, and Intersubjectivity.* Copenhagen: Museum Tusculanum Press, 2002.

Jahanbegloo, Ramin. *Conversations with Isaiah Berlin.* New York: Charles Scribner's & Sons, 1991.

Vlasta Jalušič, "Les éléments de la tradition en question. Hannah Arendt en ex-Yougoslavie et dans les États successeurs." Hannah Arendt abroad. Lectures du Monde. *Tumultes* 30 (2008): 81–108.

Jaspers, Karl. *Philosophy.* Chicago: The University of Chicago Press, 1969.

Kanellopoulos, Panagiotis. "Musical Improvisation as Action: An Arendtian Perspective." *Action, Criticism and Theory for Music Education* 6, no. 3 (2007): 97–126.

Kant, Immanuel. *Critique of Pure Reason.* London: Penguin, 2007.

Kawasaki, Osamu. "Hannah Arendt and Political Studies in Japan." In Japanese. *The Japanese Journal of Political Thought* 6 (2006): 82–109.

Leiter, Brian, and Michael Rosen, eds. *The Oxford Handbook of Continental Philosophy.* Oxford: Oxford University Press, 2007.

Moran, Dermot, *Introduction to Phenomenology.* London & New York: Routledge, 2000.

Plato. "The Simile of the Cave." Republic. Harmondsworth: Penguin, 1974.

Pitkin, Hanna. "Justice. On Relating Private and Public." *Political Theory* 9, no. 3 (1981): 327–52.

Sandel, Michael. *Justice: What's the Right Thing to Do?* New York: Farrar, Straus and Giroux, 2010.

Schorske, Carl.E. "The New Rigorism in the Human Sciences, 1940-1960." *Daedelus* 126 (Winter 1997): 289–310.

Sennett, Richard. *The Craftsman.* New Haven: Yale University Press, 2008.

Smola, Julia. "La politique sans mots. Parler et agir en Argentine dans les années 1990." Hannah Arendt abroad. Lectures du Monde. *Tumultes* 30 (2008): 215–34.

Tassin, Etienne. *Le Trésor Perdu: Hannah Arendt, l'Intelligence de l'Action Politique.* Paris: Payot, 1999.

Young-Bruehl, Elisabeth. *Hannah Arendt: For Love Of The World.* New Haven: Yale University Press, 2004.

# THE MACAT LIBRARY
# BY DISCIPLINE

## AFRICANA STUDIES

Chinua Achebe's *An Image of Africa: Racism in Conrad's Heart of Darkness*
W. E. B. Du Bois's *The Souls of Black Folk*
Zora Neale Huston's *Characteristics of Negro Expression*
Martin Luther King Jr's *Why We Can't Wait*
Toni Morrison's *Playing in the Dark: Whiteness in the American Literary Imagination*

## ANTHROPOLOGY

Arjun Appadurai's *Modernity at Large: Cultural Dimensions of Globalisation*
Philippe Ariès's *Centuries of Childhood*
Franz Boas's *Race, Language and Culture*
Kim Chan & Renée Mauborgne's *Blue Ocean Strategy*
Jared Diamond's *Guns, Germs & Steel: the Fate of Human Societies*
Jared Diamond's *Collapse: How Societies Choose to Fail or Survive*
E. E. Evans-Pritchard's *Witchcraft, Oracles and Magic Among the Azande*
James Ferguson's *The Anti-Politics Machine*
Clifford Geertz's *The Interpretation of Cultures*
David Graeber's *Debt: the First 5000 Years*
Karen Ho's *Liquidated: An Ethnography of Wall Street*
Geert Hofstede's *Culture's Consequences: Comparing Values, Behaviors, Institutes and Organizations across Nations*
Claude Lévi-Strauss's *Structural Anthropology*
Jay Macleod's *Ain't No Makin' It: Aspirations and Attainment in a Low-Income Neighborhood*
Saba Mahmood's *The Politics of Piety: The Islamic Revival and the Feminist Subject*
Marcel Mauss's *The Gift*

## BUSINESS

Jean Lave & Etienne Wenger's *Situated Learning*
Theodore Levitt's *Marketing Myopia*
Burton G. Malkiel's *A Random Walk Down Wall Street*
Douglas McGregor's *The Human Side of Enterprise*
Michael Porter's *Competitive Strategy: Creating and Sustaining Superior Performance*
John Kotter's *Leading Change*
C. K. Prahalad & Gary Hamel's *The Core Competence of the Corporation*

## CRIMINOLOGY

Michelle Alexander's *The New Jim Crow: Mass Incarceration in the Age of Colorblindness*
Michael R. Gottfredson & Travis Hirschi's *A General Theory of Crime*
Richard Herrnstein & Charles A. Murray's *The Bell Curve: Intelligence and Class Structure in American Life*
Elizabeth Loftus's *Eyewitness Testimony*
Jay Macleod's *Ain't No Makin' It: Aspirations and Attainment in a Low-Income Neighborhood*
Philip Zimbardo's *The Lucifer Effect*

## ECONOMICS

Janet Abu-Lughod's *Before European Hegemony*
Ha-Joon Chang's *Kicking Away the Ladder*
David Brion Davis's *The Problem of Slavery in the Age of Revolution*
Milton Friedman's *The Role of Monetary Policy*
Milton Friedman's *Capitalism and Freedom*
David Graeber's *Debt: the First 5000 Years*
Friedrich Hayek's *The Road to Serfdom*
Karen Ho's *Liquidated: An Ethnography of Wall Street*

John Maynard Keynes's *The General Theory of Employment, Interest and Money*
Charles P. Kindleberger's *Manias, Panics and Crashes*
Robert Lucas's *Why Doesn't Capital Flow from Rich to Poor Countries?*
Burton G. Malkiel's *A Random Walk Down Wall Street*
Thomas Robert Malthus's *An Essay on the Principle of Population*
Karl Marx's *Capital*
Thomas Piketty's *Capital in the Twenty-First Century*
Amartya Sen's *Development as Freedom*
Adam Smith's *The Wealth of Nations*
Nassim Nicholas Taleb's *The Black Swan: The Impact of the Highly Improbable*
Amos Tversky's & Daniel Kahneman's *Judgment under Uncertainty: Heuristics and Biases*
Mahbub Ul Haq's *Reflections on Human Development*
Max Weber's *The Protestant Ethic and the Spirit of Capitalism*

## FEMINISM AND GENDER STUDIES

Judith Butler's *Gender Trouble*
Simone De Beauvoir's *The Second Sex*
Michel Foucault's *History of Sexuality*
Betty Friedan's *The Feminine Mystique*
Saba Mahmood's *The Politics of Piety: The Islamic Revival and the Feminist Subject*
Joan Wallach Scott's *Gender and the Politics of History*
Mary Wollstonecraft's *A Vindication of the Rights of Woman*
Virginia Woolf's *A Room of One's Own*

## GEOGRAPHY

The Brundtland Report's *Our Common Future*
Rachel Carson's *Silent Spring*
Charles Darwin's *On the Origin of Species*
James Ferguson's *The Anti-Politics Machine*
Jane Jacobs's *The Death and Life of Great American Cities*
James Lovelock's *Gaia: A New Look at Life on Earth*
Amartya Sen's *Development as Freedom*
Mathis Wackernagel & William Rees's *Our Ecological Footprint*

## HISTORY

Janet Abu-Lughod's *Before European Hegemony*
Benedict Anderson's *Imagined Communities*
Bernard Bailyn's *The Ideological Origins of the American Revolution*
Hanna Batatu's *The Old Social Classes And The Revolutionary Movements Of Iraq*
Christopher Browning's *Ordinary Men: Reserve Police Batallion 101 and the Final Solution in Poland*
Edmund Burke's *Reflections on the Revolution in France*
William Cronon's *Nature's Metropolis: Chicago And The Great West*
Alfred W. Crosby's *The Columbian Exchange*
Hamid Dabashi's *Iran: A People Interrupted*
David Brion Davis's *The Problem of Slavery in the Age of Revolution*
Nathalie Zemon Davis's *The Return of Martin Guerre*
Jared Diamond's *Guns, Germs & Steel: the Fate of Human Societies*
Frank Dikotter's *Mao's Great Famine*
John W Dower's *War Without Mercy: Race And Power In The Pacific War*
W. E. B. Du Bois's *The Souls of Black Folk*
Richard J. Evans's *In Defence of History*
Lucien Febvre's *The Problem of Unbelief in the 16th Century*
Sheila Fitzpatrick's *Everyday Stalinism*

The Macat Library By Discipline

Eric Foner's *Reconstruction: America's Unfinished Revolution, 1863-1877*
Michel Foucault's *Discipline and Punish*
Michel Foucault's *History of Sexuality*
Francis Fukuyama's *The End of History and the Last Man*
John Lewis Gaddis's *We Now Know: Rethinking Cold War History*
Ernest Gellner's *Nations and Nationalism*
Eugene Genovese's *Roll, Jordan, Roll: The World the Slaves Made*
Carlo Ginzburg's *The Night Battles*
Daniel Goldhagen's *Hitler's Willing Executioners*
Jack Goldstone's *Revolution and Rebellion in the Early Modern World*
Antonio Gramsci's *The Prison Notebooks*
Alexander Hamilton, John Jay & James Madison's *The Federalist Papers*
Christopher Hill's *The World Turned Upside Down*
Carole Hillenbrand's *The Crusades: Islamic Perspectives*
Thomas Hobbes's *Leviathan*
Eric Hobsbawm's *The Age Of Revolution*
John A. Hobson's *Imperialism: A Study*
Albert Hourani's *History of the Arab Peoples*
Samuel P. Huntington's *The Clash of Civilizations and the Remaking of World Order*
C. L. R. James's *The Black Jacobins*
Tony Judt's *Postwar: A History of Europe Since 1945*
Ernst Kantorowicz's *The King's Two Bodies: A Study in Medieval Political Theology*
Paul Kennedy's *The Rise and Fall of the Great Powers*
Ian Kershaw's *The "Hitler Myth": Image and Reality in the Third Reich*
John Maynard Keynes's *The General Theory of Employment, Interest and Money*
Charles P. Kindleberger's *Manias, Panics and Crashes*
Martin Luther King Jr's *Why We Can't Wait*
Henry Kissinger's *World Order: Reflections on the Character of Nations and the Course of History*
Thomas Kuhn's *The Structure of Scientific Revolutions*
Georges Lefebvre's *The Coming of the French Revolution*
John Locke's *Two Treatises of Government*
Niccolò Machiavelli's *The Prince*
Thomas Robert Malthus's *An Essay on the Principle of Population*
Mahmood Mamdani's *Citizen and Subject: Contemporary Africa And The Legacy Of Late Colonialism*
Karl Marx's *Capital*
Stanley Milgram's *Obedience to Authority*
John Stuart Mill's *On Liberty*
Thomas Paine's *Common Sense*
Thomas Paine's *Rights of Man*
Geoffrey Parker's *Global Crisis: War, Climate Change and Catastrophe in the Seventeenth Century*
Jonathan Riley-Smith's *The First Crusade and the Idea of Crusading*
Jean-Jacques Rousseau's *The Social Contract*
Joan Wallach Scott's *Gender and the Politics of History*
Theda Skocpol's *States and Social Revolutions*
Adam Smith's *The Wealth of Nations*
Timothy Snyder's *Bloodlands: Europe Between Hitler and Stalin*
Sun Tzu's *The Art of War*
Keith Thomas's *Religion and the Decline of Magic*
Thucydides's *The History of the Peloponnesian War*
Frederick Jackson Turner's *The Significance of the Frontier in American History*
Odd Arne Westad's *The Global Cold War: Third World Interventions And The Making Of Our Times*

## LITERATURE

Chinua Achebe's *An Image of Africa: Racism in Conrad's Heart of Darkness*
Roland Barthes's *Mythologies*
Homi K. Bhabha's *The Location of Culture*
Judith Butler's *Gender Trouble*
Simone De Beauvoir's *The Second Sex*
Ferdinand De Saussure's *Course in General Linguistics*
T. S. Eliot's *The Sacred Wood: Essays on Poetry and Criticism*
Zora Neale Huston's *Characteristics of Negro Expression*
Toni Morrison's *Playing in the Dark: Whiteness in the American Literary Imagination*
Edward Said's *Orientalism*
Gayatri Chakravorty Spivak's *Can the Subaltern Speak?*
Mary Wollstonecraft's *A Vindication of the Rights of Women*
Virginia Woolf's *A Room of One's Own*

## PHILOSOPHY

Elizabeth Anscombe's  *Modern Moral Philosophy*
Hannah Arendt's *The Human Condition*
Aristotle's *Metaphysics*
Aristotle's *Nicomachean Ethics*
Edmund Gettier's *Is Justified True Belief Knowledge?*
Georg Wilhelm Friedrich Hegel's *Phenomenology of Spirit*
David Hume's *Dialogues Concerning Natural Religion*
David Hume's *The Enquiry for Human Understanding*
Immanuel Kant's *Religion within the Boundaries of Mere Reason*
Immanuel Kant's *Critique of Pure Reason*
Søren Kierkegaard's *The Sickness Unto Death*
Søren Kierkegaard's *Fear and Trembling*
C. S. Lewis's *The Abolition of Man*
Alasdair MacIntyre's *After Virtue*
Marcus Aurelius's *Meditations*
Friedrich Nietzsche's *On the Genealogy of Morality*
Friedrich Nietzsche's *Beyond Good and Evil*
Plato's *Republic*
Plato's *Symposium*
Jean-Jacques Rousseau's *The Social Contract*
Gilbert Ryle's *The Concept of Mind*
Baruch Spinoza's *Ethics*
Sun Tzu's *The Art of War*
Ludwig Wittgenstein's *Philosophical Investigations*

## POLITICS

Benedict Anderson's *Imagined Communities*
Aristotle's *Politics*
Bernard Bailyn's *The Ideological Origins of the American Revolution*
Edmund Burke's *Reflections on the Revolution in France*
John C. Calhoun's *A Disquisition on Government*
Ha-Joon Chang's *Kicking Away the Ladder*
Hamid Dabashi's *Iran: A People Interrupted*
Hamid Dabashi's *Theology of Discontent: The Ideological Foundation of the Islamic Revolution in Iran*
Robert Dahl's *Democracy and its Critics*
Robert Dahl's *Who Governs?*
David Brion Davis's *The Problem of Slavery in the Age of Revolution*

# The Macat Library By Discipline

Alexis De Tocqueville's *Democracy in America*
James Ferguson's *The Anti-Politics Machine*
Frank Dikotter's *Mao's Great Famine*
Sheila Fitzpatrick's *Everyday Stalinism*
Eric Foner's *Reconstruction: America's Unfinished Revolution, 1863-1877*
Milton Friedman's *Capitalism and Freedom*
Francis Fukuyama's *The End of History and the Last Man*
John Lewis Gaddis's *We Now Know: Rethinking Cold War History*
Ernest Gellner's *Nations and Nationalism*
David Graeber's *Debt: the First 5000 Years*
Antonio Gramsci's *The Prison Notebooks*
Alexander Hamilton, John Jay & James Madison's *The Federalist Papers*
Friedrich Hayek's *The Road to Serfdom*
Christopher Hill's *The World Turned Upside Down*
Thomas Hobbes's *Leviathan*
John A. Hobson's *Imperialism: A Study*
Samuel P. Huntington's *The Clash of Civilizations and the Remaking of World Order*
Tony Judt's *Postwar: A History of Europe Since 1945*
David C. Kang's *China Rising: Peace, Power and Order in East Asia*
Paul Kennedy's *The Rise and Fall of Great Powers*
Robert Keohane's *After Hegemony*
Martin Luther King Jr.'s *Why We Can't Wait*
Henry Kissinger's *World Order: Reflections on the Character of Nations and the Course of History*
John Locke's *Two Treatises of Government*
Niccolò Machiavelli's *The Prince*
Thomas Robert Malthus's *An Essay on the Principle of Population*
Mahmood Mamdani's *Citizen and Subject: Contemporary Africa And The Legacy Of Late Colonialism*
Karl Marx's *Capital*
John Stuart Mill's *On Liberty*
John Stuart Mill's *Utilitarianism*
Hans Morgenthau's *Politics Among Nations*
Thomas Paine's *Common Sense*
Thomas Paine's *Rights of Man*
Thomas Piketty's *Capital in the Twenty-First Century*
Robert D. Putman's *Bowling Alone*
John Rawls's *Theory of Justice*
Jean-Jacques Rousseau's *The Social Contract*
Theda Skocpol's *States and Social Revolutions*
Adam Smith's *The Wealth of Nations*
Sun Tzu's *The Art of War*
Henry David Thoreau's *Civil Disobedience*
Thucydides's *The History of the Peloponnesian War*
Kenneth Waltz's *Theory of International Politics*
Max Weber's *Politics as a Vocation*
Odd Arne Westad's *The Global Cold War: Third World Interventions And The Making Of Our Times*

## POSTCOLONIAL STUDIES

Roland Barthes's *Mythologies*
Frantz Fanon's *Black Skin, White Masks*
Homi K. Bhabha's *The Location of Culture*
Gustavo Gutiérrez's *A Theology of Liberation*
Edward Said's *Orientalism*
Gayatri Chakravorty Spivak's *Can the Subaltern Speak?*

## PSYCHOLOGY

Gordon Allport's *The Nature of Prejudice*
Alan Baddeley & Graham Hitch's *Aggression: A Social Learning Analysis*
Albert Bandura's *Aggression: A Social Learning Analysis*
Leon Festinger's *A Theory of Cognitive Dissonance*
Sigmund Freud's *The Interpretation of Dreams*
Betty Friedan's *The Feminine Mystique*
Michael R. Gottfredson & Travis Hirschi's *A General Theory of Crime*
Eric Hoffer's *The True Believer: Thoughts on the Nature of Mass Movements*
William James's *Principles of Psychology*
Elizabeth Loftus's *Eyewitness Testimony*
A. H. Maslow's *A Theory of Human Motivation*
Stanley Milgram's *Obedience to Authority*
Steven Pinker's *The Better Angels of Our Nature*
Oliver Sacks's *The Man Who Mistook His Wife For a Hat*
Richard Thaler & Cass Sunstein's *Nudge: Improving Decisions About Health, Wealth and Happiness*
Amos Tversky's *Judgment under Uncertainty: Heuristics and Biases*
Philip Zimbardo's *The Lucifer Effect*

## SCIENCE

Rachel Carson's *Silent Spring*
William Cronon's *Nature's Metropolis: Chicago And The Great West*
Alfred W. Crosby's *The Columbian Exchange*
Charles Darwin's *On the Origin of Species*
Richard Dawkin's *The Selfish Gene*
Thomas Kuhn's *The Structure of Scientific Revolutions*
Geoffrey Parker's *Global Crisis: War, Climate Change and Catastrophe in the Seventeenth Century*
Mathis Wackernagel & William Rees's *Our Ecological Footprint*

## SOCIOLOGY

Michelle Alexander's *The New Jim Crow: Mass Incarceration in the Age of Colorblindness*
Gordon Allport's *The Nature of Prejudice*
Albert Bandura's *Aggression: A Social Learning Analysis*
Hanna Batatu's *The Old Social Classes And The Revolutionary Movements Of Iraq*
Ha-Joon Chang's *Kicking Away the Ladder*
W. E. B. Du Bois's *The Souls of Black Folk*
Émile Durkheim's *On Suicide*
Frantz Fanon's *Black Skin, White Masks*
Frantz Fanon's *The Wretched of the Earth*
Eric Foner's *Reconstruction: America's Unfinished Revolution, 1863-1877*
Eugene Genovese's *Roll, Jordan, Roll: The World the Slaves Made*
Jack Goldstone's *Revolution and Rebellion in the Early Modern World*
Antonio Gramsci's *The Prison Notebooks*
Richard Herrnstein & Charles A Murray's *The Bell Curve: Intelligence and Class Structure in American Life*
Eric Hoffer's *The True Believer: Thoughts on the Nature of Mass Movements*
Jane Jacobs's *The Death and Life of Great American Cities*
Robert Lucac's *Why Doesn't Capital Flow from Rich to Poor Countries?*
Jay Macleod's *Ain't No Makin' It: Aspirations and Attainment in a Low Income Neighborhood*
Elaine May's *Homeward Bound: American Families in the Cold War Era*
Douglas McGregor's *The Human Side of Enterprise*
C. Wright Mills's *The Sociological Imagination*

The Macat Library By Discipline

Thomas Piketty's *Capital in the Twenty-First Century*
Robert D. Putman's *Bowling Alone*
David Riesman's *The Lonely Crowd: A Study of the Changing American Character*
Edward Said's *Orientalism*
Joan Wallach Scott's *Gender and the Politics of History*
Theda Skocpol's *States and Social Revolutions*
Max Weber's *The Protestant Ethic and the Spirit of Capitalism*

## THEOLOGY

Augustine's *Confessions*
Benedict's *Rule of St Benedict*
Gustavo Gutiérrez's *A Theology of Liberation*
Carole Hillenbrand's *The Crusades: Islamic Perspectives*
David Hume's *Dialogues Concerning Natural Religion*
Immanuel Kant's *Religion within the Boundaries of Mere Reason*
Ernst Kantorowicz's *The King's Two Bodies: A Study in Medieval Political Theology*
Søren Kierkegaard's *The Sickness Unto Death*
C. S. Lewis's *The Abolition of Man*
Saba Mahmood's *The Politics of Piety: The Islamic Revival and the Feminist Subject*
Baruch Spinoza's *Ethics*
Keith Thomas's *Religion and the Decline of Magic*

## COMING SOON

Chris Argyris's *The Individual and the Organisation*
Seyla Benhabib's *The Rights of Others*
Walter Benjamin's *The Work Of Art in the Age of Mechanical Reproduction*
John Berger's *Ways of Seeing*
Pierre Bourdieu's *Outline of a Theory of Practice*
Mary Douglas's *Purity and Danger*
Roland Dworkin's *Taking Rights Seriously*
James G. March's *Exploration and Exploitation in Organisational Learning*
Ikujiro Nonaka's *A Dynamic Theory of Organizational Knowledge Creation*
Griselda Pollock's *Vision and Difference*
Amartya Sen's *Inequality Re-Examined*
Susan Sontag's *On Photography*
Yasser Tabbaa's *The Transformation of Islamic Art*
Ludwig von Mises's *Theory of Money and Credit*

# Macat Disciplines

*Access the greatest ideas and thinkers across entire disciplines, including*

## *Postcolonial Studies*

**Roland Barthes's** *Mythologies*
**Frantz Fanon's** *Black Skin, White Masks*
**Homi K. Bhabha's** *The Location of Culture*
**Gustavo Gutiérrez's** *A Theology of Liberation*
**Edward Said's** *Orientalism*
**Gayatri Chakravorty Spivak's** *Can the Subaltern Speak?*

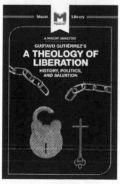

# Macat Disciplines

*Access the greatest ideas and thinkers across entire disciplines, including*

## AFRICANA STUDIES

**Chinua Achebe's** *An Image of Africa: Racism in Conrad's Heart of Darkness*

**W. E. B. Du Bois's** *The Souls of Black Folk*

**Zora Neale Hurston's** *Characteristics of Negro Expression*

**Martin Luther King Jr.'s** *Why We Can't Wait*

**Toni Morrison's** *Playing in the Dark: Whiteness in the American Literary Imagination*

Macat analyses are available from all good bookshops and libraries.

Access hundreds of analyses through one, multimedia tool.
Join free for one month **library.macat.com**

# Macat Disciplines

*Access the greatest ideas and thinkers across entire disciplines, including*

## FEMINISM, GENDER AND QUEER STUDIES

**Simone De Beauvoir's**
*The Second Sex*

**Michel Foucault's**
*History of Sexuality*

**Betty Friedan's**
*The Feminine Mystique*

**Saba Mahmood's**
*The Politics of Piety:
The Islamic Revival and
the Feminist Subject*

**Joan Wallach Scott's**
*Gender and the
Politics of History*

**Mary Wollstonecraft's**
*A Vindication of the
Rights of Woman*

**Virginia Woolf's**
*A Room of One's Own*

**Judith Butler's**
*Gender Trouble*

Macat analyses are available from all good bookshops and libraries.

Access hundreds of analyses through one, multimedia tool.

Join free for one month **library.macat.com**

# Macat Disciplines

*Access the greatest ideas and thinkers across entire disciplines, including*

## CRIMINOLOGY

**Michelle Alexander's**
*The New Jim Crow: Mass Incarceration in the Age of Colorblindness*

**Michael R. Gottfredson & Travis Hirschi's**
*A General Theory of Crime*

**Elizabeth Loftus's**
*Eyewitness Testimony*

**Richard Herrnstein & Charles A. Murray's**
*The Bell Curve: Intelligence and Class Structure in American Life*

**Jay Macleod's**
*Ain't No Makin' It: Aspirations and Attainment in a Low-Income Neighborhood*

**Philip Zimbardo's**
*The Lucifer Effect*

Macat analyses are available from all good bookshops and libraries.

Access hundreds of analyses through one, multimedia tool.
Join free for one month **library.macat.com**

# Macat Disciplines

*Access the greatest ideas and thinkers across entire disciplines, including*

## INEQUALITY

**Ha-Joon Chang's,** *Kicking Away the Ladder*

**David Graeber's,** *Debt: The First 5000 Years*

**Robert E. Lucas's,** *Why Doesn't Capital Flow from Rich To Poor Countries?*

**Thomas Piketty's,** *Capital in the Twenty-First Century*

**Amartya Sen's,** *Inequality Re-Examined*

**Mahbub Ul Haq's,** *Reflections on Human Development*

# Macat Pairs

*Analyse historical and modern issues from opposite sides of an argument. Pairs include:*

## RACE AND IDENTITY

### Zora Neale Hurston's
*Characteristics of Negro Expression*

Using material collected on anthropological expeditions to the South, Zora Neale Hurston explains how expression in African American culture in the early twentieth century departs from the art of white America. At the time, African American art was often criticized for copying white culture. For Hurston, this criticism misunderstood how art works. European tradition views art as something fixed. But Hurston describes a creative process that is alive, ever-changing, and largely improvisational. She maintains that African American art works through a process called 'mimicry'—where an imitated object or verbal pattern, for example, is reshaped and altered until it becomes something new, novel—and worthy of attention.

### Frantz Fanon's
*Black Skin, White Masks*

*Black Skin, White Masks* offers a radical analysis of the psychological effects of colonization on the colonized.

Fanon witnessed the effects of colonization first hand both in his birthplace, Martinique, and again later in life when he worked as a psychiatrist in another French colony, Algeria. His text is uncompromising in form and argument. He dissects the dehumanizing effects of colonialism, arguing that it destroys the native sense of identity, forcing people to adapt to an alien set of values—including a core belief that they are inferior. This results in deep psychological trauma.

Fanon's work played a pivotal role in the civil rights movements of the 1960s.

# Macat Pairs

*Analyse historical and modern issues from opposite sides of an argument.
Pairs include:*

# Macat Disciplines

*Access the greatest ideas and thinkers across entire disciplines, including*

## GLOBALIZATION

**Arjun Appadurai's,** *Modernity at Large: Cultural Dimensions of Globalisation*

**James Ferguson's,** *The Anti-Politics Machine*

**Geert Hofstede's,** *Culture's Consequences*

**Amartya Sen's,** *Development as Freedom*

Macat analyses are available from all good bookshops and libraries.

Access hundreds of analyses through one, multimedia tool.
Join free for one month **library.macat.com**

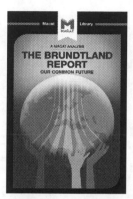

# Macat Disciplines

*Access the greatest ideas and thinkers across entire disciplines, including*

## THE FUTURE OF DEMOCRACY

**Robert A. Dahl's,** *Democracy and Its Critics*
**Robert A. Dahl's,** *Who Governs?*
**Alexis De Toqueville's,** *Democracy in America*
**Niccolò Machiavelli's,** *The Prince*
**John Stuart Mill's,** *On Liberty*
**Robert D. Putnam's,** *Bowling Alone*
**Jean-Jacques Rousseau's,** *The Social Contract*
**Henry David Thoreau's,** *Civil Disobedience*

# Macat Pairs

*Analyse historical and modern issues from opposite sides of an argument. Pairs include:*

# Macat Pairs

*Analyse historical and modern issues
from opposite sides of an argument.
Pairs include:*

## HOW TO RUN AN ECONOMY

### John Maynard Keynes's
*The General Theory OF Employment,
Interest and Money*

Classical economics suggests that market economies
are self-correcting in times of recession or depression,
and tend toward full employment and output. But
English economist John Maynard Keynes disagrees.

In his ground-breaking 1936 study *The General
Theory*, Keynes argues that traditional economics
has misunderstood the causes of unemployment.
Employment is not determined by the price of labor;
it is directly linked to demand. Keynes believes market
economies are by nature unstable, and so require
government intervention. Spurred on by the social
catastrophe of the Great Depression of the 1930s,
he sets out to revolutionize the way the world thinks

### Milton Friedman's
*The Role of Monetary Policy*

Friedman's 1968 paper changed the course of
economic theory. In just 17 pages, he demolished
existing theory and outlined an effective alternate
monetary policy designed to secure 'high employment,
stable prices and rapid growth.'

Friedman demonstrated that monetary policy plays
a vital role in broader economic stability and argued
that economists got their monetary policy wrong
in the 1950s and 1960s by misunderstanding the
relationship between inflation and unemployment.
Previous generations of economists had believed
that governments could permanently decrease
unemployment by permitting inflation—and vice versa.
Friedman's most original contribution was to show that
this supposed trade-off is an illusion that only works in
the short term.

# Macat Pairs

*Analyse historical and modern issues from opposite sides of an argument. Pairs include:*

## ARE WE FUNDAMENTALLY GOOD - OR BAD?

### Steven Pinker's
*The Better Angels of Our Nature*

Stephen Pinker's gloriously optimistic 2011 book argues that, despite humanity's biological tendency toward violence, we are, in fact, less violent today than ever before. To prove his case, Pinker lays out pages of detailed statistical evidence. For him, much of the credit for the decline goes to the eighteenth-century Enlightenment movement, whose ideas of liberty, tolerance, and respect for the value of human life filtered down through society and affected how people thought. That psychological change led to behavioral change—and overall we became more peaceful. Critics countered that humanity could never overcome the biological urge toward violence; others argued that Pinker's statistics were flawed.

### Philip Zimbardo's
*The Lucifer Effect*

Some psychologists believe those who commit cruelty are innately evil. Zimbardo disagrees. In *The Lucifer Effect*, he argues that sometimes good people do evil things simply because of the situations they find themselves in, citing many historical examples to illustrate his point. Zimbardo details his 1971 Stanford prison experiment, where ordinary volunteers playing guards in a mock prison rapidly became abusive. But he also describes the tortures committed by US army personnel in Iraq's Abu Ghraib prison in 2003—and how he himself testified in defence of one of those guards. committed by US army personnel in Iraq's Abu Ghraib prison in 2003—and how he himself testified in defence of one of those guards.

Printed in the United States
by Baker & Taylor Publisher Services